That's One Smart Puppy

The Ultimate Care Guide to Raising a
Happy, Healthy, and Obedient Puppy

Hope Chambers

Library of Congress Control Number: 2023937063

Print ISBN: 979-8-9876848-7-0

eBook ISBN: 979-8-9876848-8-7

Table of Contents

Introduction

The kids are screaming with excitement as we head to the car. After six months of begging, I finally gave in, and for her 14th birthday, my daughter Kelsey is getting the puppy of her dreams. Of course, she had no idea what puppy she wanted. At first, it was an Australian sheepdog, then it was a chihuahua, and then an Alaskan Malamute. After explaining to her that there are dogs out there that have been abandoned and some that have never had a home, to begin with, it was settled. The local shelter was where she would find her best friend.

When we arrived, we were introduced to Mama Daisy. A beautiful black and white Shih Tzu that had been abandoned. Thankfully, a local superhero had found her and brought her to the shelter, where she would be cared for and loved until her forever home was found. Surprise, surprise, Mama Daisy delivered three beautiful puppies just two days after she arrived. While she had secured a forever home with one of the employees, it was time for her babies to find theirs.

As we entered the room with the puppies, Kelsey dropped to her knees, and a little black ball of fluff ran straight into her arms. It was clear that the bond created at that moment would last a lifetime. She announced that his name was Sam, and we all agreed it suited him. We drove back home, where a new kennel, soft bed, puppy food, and tons of toys awaited our bundle of joy. The joy on their faces was enough to make me think that this was the best decision I had ever made.

Then reality hit, and as we walked in that door, little Sam turned into a terror! I would walk around the corner of the hallway, and there was Sam running with a toilet paper stream following behind. "Sam! STOP." He would glance at me for a second before running down the stairs, through the kitchen, and to the living room. The stream of paper gets longer by the second. Of course, Kelsey was off at school, and this had now become my clean-up.

Sam is a cutie for sure, his hair grew long, and Kelsey brushed him every day. She would even put a tiny little pony on top of his head to keep the hair out of his eyes. Yet, that sweet demeanor only seemed to last while she was around, and the moment she left the room, Sam would leave a puddle on the floor! Ugh!

Leaving my new leather pumps on the floor was my first mistake. Sam was teething and developed a taste for shoes of any type. Not just shoes, though, wooden chair legs did just as well, how on earth do I hide those?

The frustration set in, and I started second-guessing my decision. What have I gotten myself into? Kelsey goes to school every day and is off with her friends, playing soccer or band practice the rest of the time. Just as I finished the thought, Kelsey walked through the front door, dropping her book bag and getting down on her knees. She yelled out for Sam, and sure enough, that little fluff ball sprints down the hall and runs toward her, wiggling that little butt the entire way. That settles it. Sam can stay, but I need to step up and focus on getting this puppy trained if he wants to live through my wrath!

Puppies are a big responsibility, bigger than most people think. They don't come preprogrammed, and everything they learn, they learn from you. If you are struggling with a similar situation, whether the puppy was for you or for your child, don't worry, I have your back.

I have been studying, caring for, and training dogs for the last thirty years, and while some have brought me to the brink of madness, they have always brought me back with their unconditional love. Each of these pups has taught me valuable lessons, and every up and down brought me a little closer to understanding what they truly need.

Come along with me to learn the steps we took to turn Sam into a smart, obedient puppy.

Chapter 1:

So, You Want a Puppy…

Are You Sure You're Ready?

Dogs are spectacular, and they are just so cute, especially when they're puppies. Yet so many people seem to forget that dogs grow up, and they continue to grow up for an average of 15 years! Adopting a puppy is easy enough to do, but caring for that puppy for all those years can become difficult, especially for people who work long hours or enjoy traveling.

Before committing your time, money, and energy to a dog, you need to ensure that you are adopting them for the right reasons, not just because they are cute! So, what is your reason?

Worker Dogs

Dogs have been bred for a multitude of reasons over the years, and knowing how lazy humans can be, the first breeds we engineered were designed to do our work for us. Whether you are looking for a farm dog to help care for your livestock, a guard dog to protect your family, or a hound dog to accompany you on hunting trips, I can guarantee there is a breed for you.

These dogs have been bred for their strong instincts, but if you are looking at adopting a worker pup, you are going to have to buy a lot more books! They require rigorous training and a strict routine in order to succeed in the jobs assigned to them.

It is important to remember that just because your dog is a worker, you don't get to treat them like an employee. There is no clocking out after a hard day. They don't even get to take leave for a vacation in Hawaii. They are part of your family and need to be treated as such. Loads of snuggles, a comfortable home, and one-on-one play time are needed to maintain a strong, healthy relationship between the two of you.

Family Dogs

Got kids? Get Labradors! Just kidding, there are tons and tons of breeds with sweet, relaxed natures that are perfect for the family, no matter how young your kids may be. There is nothing more special than growing up with a loving dog, and the bond between a child and their dog is unbreakable. However, kids go to school, they go to camp, and they have sleepovers. This means that you are ultimately going to be reasonable for the care of their pup, so it's important to ensure that your relationship is just as strong.

If you are looking at adopting a puppy for your children, make sure to do research on the different breeds. While all dogs are ultimately family-friendly, depending on how you raise them, of course, there are some breeds that may not tolerate tiny tots that don't understand why they shouldn't pull ears. The last thing you want is for your dog to be harmed because your children aren't fully trained. Okay, you don't want an injured child, either.

Companions

If you are looking for somebody to comfort you, adventure with you, and spend every waking moment with you, then a dog is definitely the right choice. Companion dogs are a little more specialized than family dogs. The bond you create and the love they have for you is a selfish one, and it can be difficult for either of you to allow a third party in. There is no set breed that makes a good companion, only how you decide to train and bond with them.

Replacement Dogs

Losing a loved one or a pet can leave a terrible hole in our hearts, and regardless of what people say, adopting a new dog to fill this void is not necessarily a bad thing. Our dogs are often our life rafts when we are drowning in sorrow, and the joy they are capable of bringing back into our lives is irreplaceable. However, dogs, especially puppies, are hard work.

They make plenty of mistakes, which can be frustrating on the best of days. They are also very capable of understanding and mimicking your emotional state. If you are in a bad headspace, your dog may be too. It's important to ensure that you are in a safe emotional space to care for them, teach them and deal with their mistakes responsibly.

The Cons

Let's quickly run through the cons, although for some of you, these may count as pros too. I promise I am not trying to put you off on adopting a puppy, but you need to know what you are in for when you invite that little ball of chaos into your life.

How Far Does Your Wallet Stretch?

Money, money, money! Dogs are not cheap. You are going to need to budget appropriately to ensure that you provide them with the best care and life that you can. Dog food expenses are usually the first thing that comes to mind, especially when you find out that cheap no-brand dog food at the grocery store is not quite enough. But this is, in fact, one of the cheaper parts of owning a pooch.

Yearly veterinarian check-ups, vaccinations, parasite medications, and regular grooming can take quite a chunk out of your salary. Let's not forget that unexpected illness and injury can also wrack up quite a veterinarian bill. This is one of those in sickness or in health situations, and if you aren't prepared to provide your dog with medical care, regardless of cost, then you may need to rethink your decision.

Medical care and food are the bare minimum needed to keep your dog alive, but being alive is not enough. You are going to need toys, bedding, walking equipment, and all the other little knick-knacks that are sure to accumulate in your closet. These are not once—off expenses, especially for chewers that go through toys like candy. Be prepared to purchase replacements every couple of months!

Say Goodbye to Spare Time

This is a bit of a pro and a con, depending on your personality and lifestyle. If you like to sleep in late, get used to being an early bird. If you enjoy lounging in front of the TV. Get used to cutting your Netflix time short, it's walking time. Dogs, just like people, require attention, and while you have been at work, they have been alone and bored.

You need to understand that you are as much their companion as they are yours and treat them as such. Most dogs aren't too needy, and simply giving them a snuggle while you read your book is exciting for them.

Patience Is a Virtue

Have you ever met a person that tests your patience almost to your breaking point? You know the ones I am referring to. You find yourself gritting your teeth, counting to ten, and, occasionally, diving behind a trash can to hide when you see them in public. This is how your dog is going to make you feel.

When you stand in that puddle of pee or find your favorite shoes chewed to pieces in the living room, you may find you have actually developed a stress-related eye twitch. Thankfully, these occasions are few and far between, and the many good days are enough to cancel the feeling out, but it's important to prepare for them and find the best coping mechanism to deal with them when they happen.

The Undoubtable Pros

Hopefully, you haven't decided to throw this book in the trash and skip out on the idea of owning a dog altogether because there are some absolutely fantastic pros that will definitely outweigh the cons, over and over again.

Never Be Alone Again

This may feel a bit weird at first, having a little creature stalk your every move. Get used to zero privacy bathroom time! However, after a while, you won't actually know what to do with yourself when your pup isn't around. Dogs have a remarkable ability to provide us with unconditional love, even after we have been a bit mean to them. All that goofy goodness releases some breathtaking chemicals and hormones in our brains that greatly reduce anxiety and stress. Just the thought of arriving home to your dog can spark a reaction.

This companionship is not only unique to us. Dogs love company, and when you're not around, they can get quite lonely. If you already own a dog, it's a good idea to adopt another.

Babysitters

You probably shouldn't leave your kids at home with your dog alone, but dogs are surprisingly good teachers, and they don't even know it. Children learn a great deal of responsibility from owning a dog, and research has indicated that they actually develop cognitive, emotional, motor, and social skills quicker than children that don't own dogs.

Safety

Whether you have a giant breed or a tiny tot, dogs provide us with invaluable security. They are quick to alert you to strange sounds at night and are loyal enough to protect us to their last breath. Some breeds (with a little extra training) are even used to detect medical conditions such as seizures and can alert you before it happens.

Getting Out Of Your Comfort Zone

Exercise! We have all heard it enough times. Regular exercise keeps you mentally, emotionally, and physically healthy, but just how many of us actually get off the couch and do it? Puppies require regular walks, playtime, and sunshine and when they don't get it, you will suffer the consequences. And by consequences, I mean a destroyed house!

Getting out will not just benefit your health, it is also a great way to meet new people and make some friends. There are not many people who can resist stopping to pet a cute dog.

Science Says So

The researchers have spoken, and we must listen. There are some remarkable studies that have been done on just how beneficial owning a dog can actually be. Other than ensuring we exercise and regularly lifting our spirits, dogs can actually reduce health issues. It's been found that pet owners, especially seniors, had a 50% reduction in health problems. If that's not enough, it has also been found that people who have suffered from major surgeries or illnesses recover much quicker if they own a pet (Carr et al., 2019). Talk about a reason to live!

Your Lifestyle Matters

If you have gotten this far, your mind is clearly made up, you are getting a dog! Now you need to decide which kind of dog will best suit you. Read through this section carefully. Even if you already have a breed in mind, they might not actually work with your lifestyle. It's best to compromise before you invite a dog into your life that you can't actually care for.

Housing

This should not really require an explanation, but shelters all around the world have proven me wrong. Around 18% of the pets currently in shelters have been surrendered because of their owners' housing situation (Weiss et al., 2015). This may not seem like a lot, but let's do the math. The ASPCA estimates that around 6.3 million pets are surrendered each year in the United States alone (ASPCA, 2022). That means that 1.13 million pets have been dropped off at shelters because of housing issues. Be smarter, and be better.

If you are not in a secure housing situation or if you have plans to move to another country, don't adopt a dog. If you live in an apartment, regardless of how many walks you think you can have a day, do not adopt a big dog. If you live on a large property, you're in luck, you can have your pick of the litter!

Fitness Levels

We have already spoken about how your new pup is going to transform you from a couch potato to an Olympic gold medalist. However, if you know that you won't be able to stick to a constant exercise routine, it's best to choose a couch potato breed. Siberian huskies are gorgeous and are often on the top of most adoption lists, but not many owners can actually handle them. They require at least an hour and a half of exercise a day, and most of that should be focused on running.

In comparison, an adorable droopy-eyed basset hound needs around two 20-minute walks a day and a calm play session. See what I am getting at? Don't overestimate your abilities.

Fur Alert!

Dogs have fur, dogs shed their fur, and you vacuum it up. It seems pretty simple and easy enough to handle, but some dogs have *a lot* of fur. I mean a lot. Even with regular grooming sessions, you will need to regularly brush them and vacuum your house daily. If you are a bit of a neat freak or somebody that suffers from allergies, this may not work in your favor. In that case, it's probably best to avoid the urge to adopt a Burmese Mountain Dog and opt for a short-haired terrier instead.

Do You Want a Worker?

The idea of a working dog is great, but it requires a lot of commitment and a strict routine to actually train them for their jobs. If you are looking at adopting a dog for security reasons, pick your breed wisely and find a professional training facility that can assist you in training them correctly.

Dogs that work medical jobs, such as leading the blind or detecting different medical conditions should be adopted from approved breeding and training facilities only. Do not risk your or your family's lives by thinking you are capable of training them to that degree.

Herders and hunting dogs, on the other hand, are surprisingly easy to train as their natural instincts kick in almost immediately. This can sometimes become an issue if you do adopt a herding breed but don't give them a job to do. If your border collie becomes bored enough, don't be surprised if you find them herding up the neighborhood kids.

Adopt or Shop?

In a perfect world, we wouldn't even have shelters. All the dogs would already be in a warm, loving home. Sadly, it's not a perfect world, and shelters have had to open as a consequence of humanity's lack of responsibility. There are plenty of misconceptions about shelters, and people often think that the dogs there are scruffy, ill-looking beasts, and the others have been thrown away for being aggressive or naughty.

There may be one or two Lady and the Tramp-looking characters there (not that looks make dogs any less deserving of love), but the vast majority are beautiful, healthy, and loving. They just need a second chance at life.

Simply put, if you have the choice, adopt!

Rescue Dog Considerations

Rescuing an adult dog from a shelter is not for the faint-hearted, and you can never be quite sure what you will get. Especially ones that have had to deal with years of trauma. Luckily, puppies are much, much easier. While many of them may have been subjected to some kind of trauma, they are still in their developmental stages, and it does not take much more than a loving home to build their confidence.

Always ask the shelter if they can provide you with a background for your pup. It's not always possible, but they will at least be able to provide you with a medical certificate. This kind of history may not seem important now, but if anything had to go wrong, medically or behaviorally, with your dog in the future, these records will help you and your veterinarian to figure out the cause.

Mixed Breeds

There is nothing that I love more than a mixed-breed dog! My oldest dog is a gorgeous brindle mix, and whenever somebody asks me what he is, I simply say, "A bit of sugar, spice, and everything nice." However, there are always pros and cons to everything.

Mixed breeds are like a box of chocolates, you never know what you will get! This could be taken as a pro or a con. They have diverse personalities and skill sets, which can be very exciting for the adventurous owner and a little disappointing for those who have high expectations. Just because they look like they have a bit of Labrador in them does not mean that they will act like one.

One of the biggest pros is that they are less likely to suffer from genetic disorders due to their colorful gene pool. The chances of behavioral issues and general medical issues are also lower as no inbreeding has taken place.

Pure Breeds

What you see is (almost) always what you get. Whether you're adopting them for their skills, beauty, or personalities, by keeping the gene pool "clean," dogs will retain their classic breed traits.

Unfortunately, there is always a con. Purebreds can suffer from genetic disorders and, in some cases, behavioral issues due to inbreeding. Most of these disorders are breed-specific, and while they can be avoided through correct breeding, it's important to be aware of them! If you intend to shop for a purebred, you will need to choose your breeder wisely and ensure that they can provide you with a full genetic and medical history for your pup.

Dog Breeds

Dogs can essentially be split up into seven categories based on what they were bred to do. Learning a bit more about each of these groups and the unique breeds will hopefully help you to find which dog will suit you best.

The Hard Workers

The working group contains some of the oldest dog breeds in history. These pups were bred for hard labor in even harder conditions. So, it is of no surprise that they are incredibly strong and generally large. Alaskan malamutes and Siberian huskies are the original sled pullers, but St. Bernards, Bernese mountain dogs, and even rottweilers all played a role in pulling carts. Other members of the working group, such as Great Danes, boxers, and Dobermans, are a little less stocky and a bit more agile and have mainly been used as farm and family protection.

Despite some of their looks (looking at you, boxers), they are all highly intelligent, which makes them easy to train but harder to keep busy. These dogs need constant mental and physical stimulation to keep them happy. Thanks to their protective and loyal natures, they all make great companions and can readily fit into any family.

The Herders

Herding dogs work just as hard, if not more, than their working group counterparts. As the name suggests, they were bred to herd and move sheep and cattle. This requires a great deal of intelligence, energy, and agility. Some breeds include border collies, German shepherds, and English sheepdogs. While they make great family pets, they generally prefer to pledge their loyalty to a single owner, and once you have been chosen, there is no escaping.

Herding breeds are arguably the most intelligent breeds in the dog kingdom. This is why many of them are still used as working dogs today, with the German shepherd dominating the police force and search and rescue teams.

The only downside to owning a herder is their never-ending energy. Seriously, have you ever seen a tired border collie? This can become problematic, especially if they don't have a job to focus their energy on. One of the best ways to relieve this pent-up energy is by getting your pup involved in agility training.

The Sporters

The sporting group was bred to be the ultimate hunting assistants. While they don't necessarily hunt themselves, they are experts at locating and retrieving game. Ever wonder why Labradors love water? It's because they were bred too.

Retrievers and Brittanys were used to retrieve waterfowl from lakes and ponds during a hunt. They don't mind getting soaked because they have specialized water-resistant fur. While they are skinny-dipping, the pointers, spaniels, and setters are on the move and doing what they do best, pointing out hidden wildlife.

These dogs form strong bonds with their companions, so much so that you will start to wonder if they can actually read your mind. Their soft natures and fun-loving personalities make them good family pets, and they are particularly fond of children. These are outdoor dogs, and cooping them up in a house all day usually doesn't end well. If you decide to adopt one, make sure that you have the space and yard for them.

The Sniffers

Oh, the hounds! Hounds are incredibly diverse in their looks, abilities, and personalities. On one hand, you have the sight hounds, which are built for speed. They are lightweight, agile dogs that can run at the speed of light to catch anything that moves. On the other hand, you have scent hounds, which are short, stocky dogs that can't seem to keep their noses off the ground. They may not be able to catch the target, but they can track it for miles.

The most notable sight hounds include greyhounds, whippets, and Irish wolfhounds. These dogs have an exceptionally high prey drive and are loaded with energy. It's important to train your dog in recall from an early age, especially if you intend to take them for regular walks and hikes. Greyhounds can run up to 45 m/h (Greyhound W. 2020), and you really don't want to be on the other side of that leash when they catch sight of a rabbit.

Our drooping-eyed, short-legged scent hounds are just as special but less likely to take you for a run when you least expect it. Basset hounds, bloodhounds, and Beagles are the most popular breeds. If you have one of these, you can expect long, slow walks. Not because they are lazy but because they are taking in an incredible amount of information through their noses.

All hounds make good companions, but some are a little more child-friendly than others. If you are looking for a family dog, opt for a calmer basset over a prey-driven greyhound.

The Lapdogs

This group contains the teacups, toys, and mini breeds. While they have been bred for a variety of reasons, they currently hold two critical roles in society. Being attentive companions and looking fabulous while doing it.

They make up for their tiny size with their explosive, sometimes stubborn personalities. They are incredibly loyal and will put up a strong fight to protect their owner until the bitter end. The most famous toy breeds include Chihuahuas, pugs, shih tzus, and Pomeranians. Their size and outgoing personalities make it easy for them to fit into any lifestyle, making them popular options for owners that live in apartments and seniors that are unable to handle larger breeds.

While toy breeds make great family dogs, their small size does make them vulnerable to heavy-handed children and larger dogs that like to play rough. Don't let their small size fool you into thinking they are low-maintenance dogs. They still require regular grooming and a good exercise routine. The only difference is that their little legs don't need to walk too far to get their steps in.

The Protectors

The terrier group are the ultimate protectors. They are hardy dogs, with the first short-legged terriers being bred to dig up rodent holes and protect homesteads from rat invasion. Long-legged terriers were later used for hunting small game.

Sadly, some terriers were bred purely for entertainment. Staffordshire bull terriers, pit bull terriers, and Spanish bull terriers were all originally bred for bull baiting and blood sport after the English bulldog was found to be too slow. Thankfully, we have moved past this dreadful part of history, and instead of shunning these breeds, we have welcomed them with open arms. Staffy's are now one of the top choices for family and child-friendly dogs! It is quite spectacular what a bit of love can do.

The smaller terriers, such as Jack Russels and Boston terriers, double as the perfect lap dogs. A warm blanket and continuous cuddles are all they need to keep them happy. All terriers are high-energy and incredibly playful. Sometimes, too playful, and their stubborn nature can come out if playtime is ended early. They are companion-driven and prefer to stick by their owners' side. Fiercely loyal and alert, these pooches will do what it takes to protect their family.

Everything In Between

Last, but certainly not least, we have the non-sporter group. This diverse group consists of all the dogs, too unique to fit into any specific category. They were bred for a variety of reasons, but most of those jobs have become redundant, and many are now used for dog shows.

Believe it or not, the royal and ever-so-cheeky poodle was once used to retrieve birds from the water. The high-energy and ever-playful dalmatian was once used to pull carts and hunt, while others, such as the aloof yet loyal chow chows, were used for anything and everything. Some held higher positions, with the Pikaneese receiving the title of royal sentinel. That explains the attitude! A few of these breeds are still used for work, but most have retired and become loving companions and simply enjoy the comforts of home life.

It's very difficult to go into the temperaments and skill sets of this group as it consists of so many breeds. It's best to research each one separately if you intend to adopt.

Chapter 2:

Preparing For Chaos

This title may be misleading and a little exaggerated (or is it?) but it's always best to prepare for the worst and be pleasantly surprised! Before you bring your puppy home, you will need to make some modifications to accommodate them. Try to think of it as bringing home a two-year-old child. You wouldn't give them free access to your pool, right? Well, I hope not, at least.

Your puppy is in a vital developmental stage, both mentally and physically, and they generally learn by watching their moms and through trial and error. Trial and error become a bit problematic when they want to know what would happen if they chew a bottle of bleach. It's important to create a safe environment for them to survive and thrive. Your puppy's perceived death wish is not the only thing you need to prepare for. If you don't have children and haven't owned a puppy before, you have to get ready for your life to turn upside down. You can try to keep your house the way it is, but it's inevitable that you will end up having toys scattered from one end to another.

Creating a Puppy Play Zone

In order to keep your house in some sort of order, you should figure out where you can make a puppy play zone. The size of this area and how you fence it off are going to depend on your puppy. When indoors, your living room is usually your best bet, and if you have a yard and a porch, I suggest you create one there as well.

There are a couple of ways to fence off these areas. Crates will be used as a resting area for your pup. However, you can purchase add-ons to these crates, which are open on the top and can be extended to the size you want, much like a fence. You can also purchase actual puppy playpens. These are typically made from a fabric mesh, but you can purchase metal ones as well.

You can use these as long-term playpens for small dog breeds, and they are especially important if you give your small puppy unsupervised time in the yard.

For larger dogs, I recommend using baby gates to confine them to a room of your choosing. I truly love baby gates and still use them today. They are a great way to still have visual contact with your dog, but they keep certain rooms in your house free of fur and mud. My living room has a door that leads to an enclosed porch and the yard. I use a baby gate that closes access off to the rest of the house. During the day, my puppies have access to the living room, porch, and, when supervised (as puppies), the yard.

Obviously, everyone's house is set up in different ways, so you will need to figure out what works best for you. If you are happy with your entire house as a playpen, that's fine too! Once you have set up your space, you will need to clear it of all things dangerous and then load it up with all things fun. Which means toys, toys, toys! So many toys!

Chew toys, squeaky toys, balls, puzzles, and stuffed toys. We will run through the different types of toys and what each one is used for. However, for now, just remember that dogs are all different, which means that they love different types of toys. I suggest that you buy one of each kind for your puppy to start with so that you can figure out which ones they enjoy the most.

Feeding Areas

I prefer for my dogs to eat their meals in a different room, and I usually choose the kitchen or dining room. I like to do this because I find that it lessens the chances of them food guarding and begging, and it allows us both to stick to a routine.

Dogs should not have free access to food all day, especially puppies that don't know when to stop! Set meals allow you to monitor their daily intake of food, and if you have a multi-pet household, it stops one dog from being a glutton while the others starve. It is much more hygienic to do this, as it stops flies and ants from invading your home. Your dog should have access to water, regardless of where they are. Have a bowl of water outside, in their play area, and in their feeding area. Dogs are resourceful, and if they don't have a water bowl outside, don't be shocked to find them in the bird bath.

Resting Areas

Resting areas are typically set up in their play areas, but I prefer three. A dog house outside, a crate in my living room, and a bed in my bedroom. My dogs quickly learn that once they get into the bedroom, the lights go off, and it's time for bed.

Dog Beds

When choosing a bed, do yourself a favor and pick one of the more expensive options. The foam in the cheaper ones breaks up quickly, and your dog ends up sleeping on the hard floor. A good quality bed will last years, and you won't need to replace it repeatedly.

Puppies grow like beanstalks, so make sure you buy one that will fit their adult size. When they are smaller, you can wrap a couple of blankets around the sides to make the bed smaller and cozier. Speaking of blankets, these are more important than you might think. Puppies aren't quite capable of regulating their body temperature properly, which means that they can get cold real quick. A good fluffy blanket will remedy this, and if you live in a cold area or one that has regular snowfall, I suggest that you buy a heated pad. These come in a variety of sizes, and you can slip them under your dog's bed. It's easy to set the temperature, and your dog will enjoy a very comfortable sleep.

Crates and Dog Houses

If your dog will be spending time outdoors while you are at work, you will need to put up a kennel with a dog house or have a fenced yard with a dog house. The most common dog houses are wooden, but if they are poorly made, they don't last long. The wood often rots, and it is very difficult to clean them. Plastic dog houses are much more hygienic and are light enough to be moved around. Make sure to keep the house undercover and out of direct sunlight so that your dog doesn't end up like beef jerky!

Crates are not for everyone, and that is understandable. It can take a bit of time to get your dog used to them. However, if you are keen on crate training, it's best to set one up before your puppy arrives and start training them immediately.

Warning! Puppy Dangers!

Alright, let's get into puppy dangers. Puppies are a bit stupid… Well, let's say they are still learning. Although some dogs never seem to stop "learning." You will need to take matters into your hands and remove any dangerous items from their reach.

Household Cleaners

Yes, they will actually attempt this. I have found my puppy with its head in my laundry detergent powder and another casually chewing on my bath soap. Thankfully, neither occasion ended badly, regardless of the panicked emergency vet visit and a massive bill. It's not just solid cleaners that you need to watch out for. Any liquid cleaners that spill can become a very deadly juice to a puppy that tries to lap it up.

Rodent and ant poisons are specially designed to be tasty enough to attract their prey. This smell will likely lure your dog in as well. There is no way to know the survival rate of a dog that has eaten poison, regardless of how quickly you get them to the vet. If you regularly use these poisons, it is best to ditch them and deal with your problem in a more natural way.

Chewables

Smart dogs won't chew foreign objects. Reasonable dogs will chew something up and leave it in bits. Yet, there are also those dogs that are stupid enough—sorry, "learning"—to chew something up and swallow those bits. Any sharp plastic pieces can actually cut through your dog's gastrointestinal tract, leading to numerous health issues and stomach ulcers. Soft pieces of fluff or fabrics can cause a buildup and blockage in the intestines, which in some cases require surgery to remove. I have been there and done that when my dog decided to eat the lining of a tennis ball. You really don't want to have to deal with it!

The problem is, you won't know that your dog is this kind of chewer until you catch them in the act. If you find something that has been chewed up, make sure that you can actually see the pieces on the floor. If you don't, monitor your pet carefully, and if you see any signs of discomfort, take them to the vet immediately. Chewing and swallowing inedible items is not only bad for the stomach, but it can also be straight-up dangerous. Puppies may chew on live wires or even batteries. Try to keep items like this out of their reach.

Escape Artists

Toy dogs are the usual suspects here. They can't seem to help but squeeze through those little gaps. It gets to the point that they are honestly just showing off to irritate you. This is one of the main reasons why you should use an outdoor playpen for unsupervised small dogs. You will also need to walk around and secure your fence. Making sure to block up any sneaky holes at the bottom.

That being said, larger dogs are not innocent either. Every now and then, one of the giant breeds figures out that they can actually scale that baby gate or fence pretty easily. This usually comes down to having manners and proper training but can occur if your dog suffers from separation anxiety. We will cover how to solve these issues a little later in the book.

Danger Zones

You may think that all dogs can swim, and while most can, your stockier breeds are much less adept. Especially if they have never been in a pool before. Puppies are full of energy but don't really have the stamina needed to paddle to the stairs if they fall in the deep end. Some don't have the height to stand on those stairs and jump out. If you have a pool, it's a good idea to put a pool cover on it when not in use. Swimming lessons are also important and can be a lifesaver in some situations.

Have you seen how uncoordinated puppies are? Some literally fall when they are just trying to walk straight. They also seem to have no spacial awareness and will likely not even realize the stairs are there until it's too late! Baby gates work well to keep your dog from going up or down the stairs, and for the first week or so, depending on their age, you should be carrying them up and down. Once they get a little older, walk up and down with them and be ready to catch them if they tumble. Trial and error.

Puppies like to believe that they are Christopher Columbus reincarnated but lack the common sense and skill set to survive in the dangerous world. If your front door leads directly to the road, do not leave it open! Even if you think that your puppy is safely confined to their play area, do not leave it open! When you are outside on walks, your puppy should always be on a leash, but don't think they won't walk off the sidewalk into the road if you are not watching. They will learn, but it can take a bit of time.

Not Even the Garden is Safe Anymore

We already know that puppies are chewers and will taste test anything that they come across. So, it's no surprise that once they are out in the garden, they will take a bite of the first juicy green they spot. In most cases, this is harmless, and once they realize it doesn't taste that great, they won't try it again.

Don't forget about pesticides and poisons. If you regularly spray your garden with pesticides or your grass with weed killer, you can poison your dog. Ditch these products and find a healthier way to deal with the problem.

These are just a few of the plants that are poisonous to dogs. If you have these in your yard, I suggest that you pull them out or keep them out of your pup's reach.

Absolute No, No's	Toxic but Not Deadly in Small Doses	Not Toxic but Certainly Not Good
Aconitum (Wolfsbane)	Belladonna	Asparagus Fern
Daffodils	Hydrangeas	Lilies
Delphinium (Larkspur)	Ivy	Hyacinths
Foxglove	Laburnum	Lupine

Absolute No, No's	Toxic but Not Deadly in Small Doses	Not Toxic but Certainly Not Good
Hemlock	Lily of the Valley	Sweet Pea
Oleander	Rhubarb	Tulips
Rhododendrons	Geraniums	Umbrella Plants
Wisteria	Peace Lilies	Poinsettias
Yew Trees	Philodendrons	Mint
Aloe Vera	Morning Glory	Parsley

It is completely normal for dogs to occasionally chew on grass, as it aids in digestion. This is not something you need to be concerned about, but it's a great idea to purchase and plant specialized pet grass, which is safe for them to chew and a lot more tasty than regular grass.

Prepping Your Family

Make sure your family is on board with you adopting a dog. You may be the one doing all the work, but if your spouse doesn't want a puppy, they are bound to get annoyed when the puppy does something wrong. Your puppy can feel the tension, so don't subject them to it.

Parenting Style

Once everyone is on board, you are going to need to pick your parenting style, and all of you will need to stick to it. There are essentially three to choose from. Authoritative, Authoritarian, and

Permissive. Permissive parenting means you let your dog do what it wants and when it wants. This is not really a good style to start off with, as puppies aren't excellent at thinking for themselves just yet and can get into plenty of harmful situations. Authoritarian parenting is very strict and demanding on a dog. It involves punishment for negative behaviors and very little reward for good ones. If you want a dog that obeys your every command but is absolutely petrified of you, then this is the style to pick. Just kidding, please don't pick this one.

Authoritative parents are more in tune with their dogs and can judge the best approach for each situation. This type of parenting involves nipping bad behaviors in the bud by reinforcing the good ones. Dogs that grow up in this kind of household are found to be much more balanced in general.

Then there is the bad cop, good cop parenting style. When you are the good one who lets the dog sleep on the couch, and your spouse is the horrible one for shouting at them to get off. This has never worked, won't work, and will never work. This creates a fragile relationship with one owner and a manipulative one with the other. Never mind the confusion your dog is going through. They never quite learn what is good or bad, they just learn how to not get caught.

Training Your Kids

Yep, I am serious! You need to train your children before you can train your dog. First things first, your kids need to stick to the parenting style and training that you use for your dog. If you don't want your dog to have human foods, ensure that your kids aren't sneaking them scraps under the table. While this seems harmless, dogs learn quickly, and don't be surprised when they start snatching food straight out of your child's mouth.

Secondly, you have to teach your children how to correctly handle and play with a dog. It's pretty simple for us, but kids have the attention span of a puppy and should be reminded often. Pulling a dog's tail or ears, barking or screaming in their face, and sticking your fingers in their eyes, or worse places will likely end up with somebody being nipped.

This happens way too often, and dogs are readily rehomed for it. Even though, let's be honest, it wasn't their fault for reacting appropriately to something painful. If you notice that your puppy avoids your children at all costs, then they have likely hurt them accidentally. You need to address this immediately and help mend their relationship to keep them both happy.

Chapter 3:

Too Late To Turn Back Now

The day is finally here, your puppy is on his way. The excitement is unbelievable, and everyone has caught the happy giggles. You walk him through the door, and you can't help but want to kiss and hug him. Except, your kids do too, and now your spouse is at it, and your mother drove from out of state to meet the little one. Suddenly, your pup is being passed around like a volleyball!

This is not really the first impression you want to make, and it's not the best way to introduce a scared little pup to a scary new space. As hard as it is for those around you, you are going to need to keep your puppy to yourself, at least for the first few hours. Introduce them to each room quietly and calmly before bringing the family in.

Once the introductions are over and your puppy is comfortable, you will need to begin your very first training routine. This includes basic household etiquette. Basically, the two of you are going to work really hard at protecting your carpets from pee.

Listen to Your Puppy!

Dogs are superb at communicating how they feel through body language. Unfortunately, we aren't good at actually reading this body language and making the right decisions based on it. It's important to understand what your puppy wants and how they feel, especially in social situations. Dogs have different thresholds, the same way that we do. This could be a pain, patience, emotional or fear-based threshold. When they reach it, their main priority will be to protect themselves.

Puppies are new to this world and have spent most of their time with their mom and littermates, learning dog socialization. They are still trying to figure out this human interaction thing, and too much "love" can overwhelm them, causing them to react negatively toward us or become scared to engage with us.

Keeping your puppy below this threshold, and giving them an opportunity to relax and recuperate when they start to reach it, is the safest way to introduce them.

Basic Body Language

We will talk about body language in more depth in the chapters to come, but for now, let's discuss the basics. A happy puppy is one that runs toward you in clear excitement. Their tongues are out and lolling about, and their tails are wagging so hard it looks like they are doing a terrible hula dance. Playful puppies will typically bounce as they walk and readily jump up onto your lap or lick you if they get the chance.

When to Stop

It's time to stop if your puppy is trying to get away from you. If they are trying to push out of your arms or keep jumping off your lap to walk to the next room, they have had enough. They may cower and try to make themselves as small as possible. If you don't listen and keep attempting to force your love on them, they will growl or attempt to nip you. This can really put a damper on the situation, but at the end of the day, you caused it. This nipping is not naughty or aggressive. Remember, puppies haven't learned human manners yet, and this is a perfectly acceptable behavior in the dog world.

Time to Meet the Family

It's best to introduce your puppy to their new home first. Place them in a calm, quiet room and show them their beds, toys, and water bowls. It's doubtful that they are going to take any interest in these things at first. They are probably ignoring you, much to your dismay, and running around sniffing their new environment. Give them the opportunity to do this, and don't be upset when they pass out in their beds immediately after. This has been a big day and that little dog can only take so much excitement.

Once they are comfortable and know where the good places to hide are, you can start bringing your family in to meet them! This is not the right time for cuddles, and it's best if everyone sits on the floor calmly and speaks softly. If you want to give your puppy some extra motivation, introduce some treats. If your puppy approaches somebody, give them permission to stroke and speak to them and if the puppy reacts excitedly, they can go in for a hug.

Again, it's likely that your pup is going to pass out after this interaction and if somebody wants to take the opportunity to snuggle them while they sleep, go for it. As long as he is still happy and doesn't try to run away, you are all good.

Is This a Crate or a Prison?

Using a crate is a debatable subject and while some people swear by it, others will flat out refuse to even play with the idea. The thing is, a crate is an incredibly helpful training tool as long as you learn to use it correctly. Confining your puppy to their crate when you are tired of dealing with them is not okay. If you treat the crate as a prison, you can be sure that this little inmate will do everything in their power to avoid serving their sentence.

Choose Your Crate

First off, pick your material. The most common crates are made from metal mesh. These seem uncomfortable, but if you buy the right size, they are often the best ones to use. They provide ventilation and sunlight, and your dog won't feel as claustrophobic. You can also buy plastic or wooden crates. Plastic and wooden ones are sealed, and you will need to ensure that they are big enough and provide enough ventilation. Plastic is definitely best for an indoor situation, as it is much easier to clean if your puppy has a potty accident. Trying to get the pee smell out of the wood in your living room will drive you to madness.

Puppies and seniors seem to prefer enclosed crates, as this quiet, dark space gives them a sense of security and a moment to get away from the world. This, however, is going to depend on your dog's personality, and while I highly recommend these for seniors, it can be pricey to buy your puppy two different crates. If you want to provide them with a bit of privacy, save your money and throw a few heavy blankets over your mesh cage to mimic the feeling.

Another money-saving tip is to buy a crate that is going to fit your dog when they are fully grown. This will also work in your favor during training as a larger crate allows your puppy more room to play, and they will be more likely to use it. Adjustable crates are also a great option but can become costly.

Once you have the crate set up, make it cozy! A thick mattress or blanket should be used to line the bottom, and throw in a couple of toys to keep your dog busy.

Crate Training

Crate training is easy enough if you are capable of self-control. Don't be surprised if your puppy cries or moans during the first few tries. Hold in the urge to rush to their rescue. They are master manipulators and will learn that a few tears will get them the freedom and attention that they want.

Step One: Comfort First

Lure your puppy into the crate with toys. Once they are in, give them plenty of treats and get them excited about being in the crate by using vocal rewards such as "Good boy/girl!" Don't close the door just yet, and if they come out, it's no biggie, you have all the time in the world.

At this age, they are still a bit insecure and much prefer being as close to their protector as possible. It can take some time for them to feel comfortable being alone. This is when covering your crate, at least two of the sides work well.

Step Two: Keep Calm, This is Just a Drill

It's time to work on closing the door. Sit calmly next to the crate and let them settle in with one of their toys. As hard as it's going to be, try not to pay any attention to them at this point. Read a book or play a game on your phone if you have to. If you concentrate too hard on the situation, they will know that something is up and anticipate a change.

Close the door about halfway and wait. They are probably going to give you the evil eye and push the door open again. If that happens, wait for them to relax and try again. If they sit calmly for a minute or so without pushing the door. Reward them! It's best to do this through the side of the crate, as rewarding them at the door may motivate them to walk out.

Step Three: Braving The Door

Closing the door. You're going to repeat the steps above, but take a deep breath, protective parents, this time, you will close the door completely. The sound of the latch will alert them immediately, and they may start crying and trying to push their way out. Sit next to the crate, but do not pay any attention to them. The moment they stop crying or move away from the door, treat them!

Remember, you are trying to reward them for being calm and relaxed in the crate. If you panic and open up the door or treat them too early, you are teaching them that freaking out is the right behavior.

Don't confine your puppy for too long. Give them a couple of minutes and open the door again. Keep repeating this throughout the day until they feel comfortable with the door closed.

Step Four: Evacuation

This is the scariest step for us. It's time to leave the room. It's best to do this when they can sit in the crate calmly for at least ten minutes. Use the steps above as usual, but this time you are going to leave the room. If they cry, you will need to ignore them until they calm down. Once calm, enter the room again, treat them, and open the crate door. Short sessions are best, and you can slowly increase their time in the crate when you are sure they are comfortable.

Oops, I Did it Again

Housebreaking your puppy should be your first priority. Potty mistakes are definitely the most infuriating part of puppy ownership. Even if they don't annoy you now, they will later when their bladders are much bigger. Don't forget: Your puppy is not behaving badly when they use your carpet as a toilet. How on earth are they supposed to know that they should be going outside? If anything, they think they have made the best decision by using the carpet because their pee won't spread to their bed or the rest of the house.

If your dog doesn't know that they have done something wrong, how can you punish them? The idea that rubbing your dog's nose in their pee will stop them from going inside is a myth. Your puppy isn't able to make that association! The only thing they learn from this punishment is that pottying at anytime, anywhere, is bad.

When they need to go potty, they are going to sneak as far away from you as possible to avoid the consequences. So don't be shocked when you find stinky presents in hidden places.

Making a Potty Area

First thing is first, puppies have tiny bladders. At this age, they will need to pee every 1–2 hours. Yep, that's 12–24 pees a day. That means that no matter how many times you take them for walks or let them outside, they will probably end up peeing in the house. If you aren't prepared to wake up in the middle of the night, then a potty area is even more of a priority. Choose one spot in your house to avoid confusion and extra clean-ups. The best place for this is in their play area.

Potty Pads

These are large absorbent pads that you can lay on the floor. Most puppies will readily take to using them for their business. For larger puppies, I suggest laying down a few or putting some newspaper underneath to avoid any leaks.

Whenever you catch your pup using one, reward them with a treat so that they understand that what they have done is good. Once they use the training pads regularly, you should stop rewarding them for it, as it can interfere with your outdoor training. Stopping the treats won't discourage them from using the pads, but it will encourage them to potty outside, as they will soon learn that that experience is more rewarding.

You won't need to use these pads forever. They are simply an outlet for your puppy when they are unable to hold it in any longer. As your dog gets older, they will be able to control their bladders better and notify you when they need to go outside.

If your pup misses the target or ends up pottying somewhere else in the house, just let it go. Clean it up, and move on! If you continue to reward them for using their training pads, they will get the point, and the mistakes will stop.

Training

Potty training is really, really easy. All you need is a bag of treats, an outdoor area, and a ton of enthusiasm. The first step will be creating a routine. It's easy to avoid mistakes if you give them enough time outside to do their business. The first potty break should be the moment you wake up. The second, after breakfast, and then every 1–2 hours until bedtime.

This is not possible for everyone, which is why the potty pads end up so important. As they get older, you will be able to extend the time between the breaks. Once your pup has full bladder control, they need to go outdoors at least four times a day. Anything over six hours will guarantee a mistake or a bladder infection.

Dogs learn best through positive reinforcement and association. If you go wild with excitement and reward them when they potty outside, they will learn this a good behavior.

I like to use a cue word for training, and before we go outside, I say, "Let's go potty!" The moment they finish their business, I make a massive deal out of it and give them several treats. This way, they can make the association between the word, the act, my happiness, and the reward.

The rewards are temporary and are only used to reinforce the good behavior until it is fully ingrained in their minds. Once they are fully potty-trained, you can stop the treats and just use vocal rewards.

Chapter 4:

Healthy Puppy, Happy Puppy

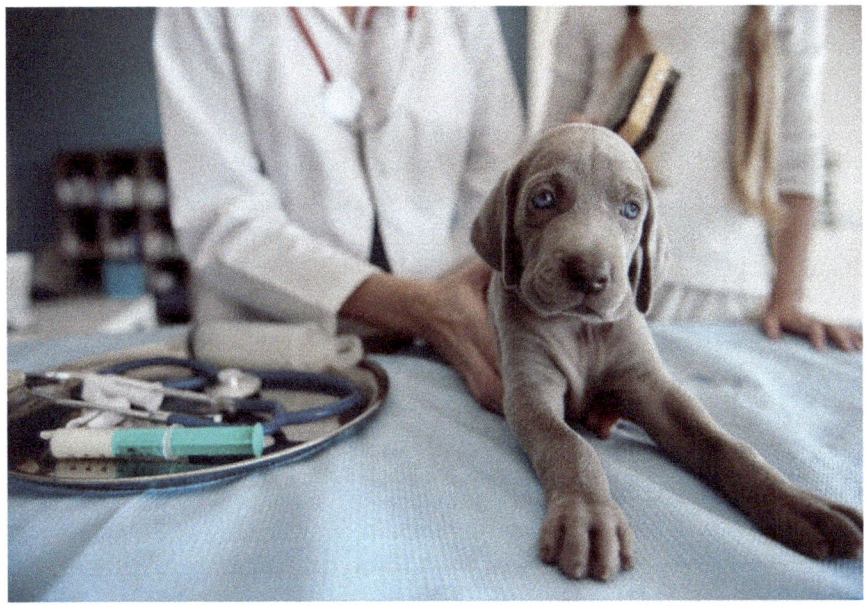

The best way to cure your puppy of an illness is by making sure that they never catch it in the first place. This is done through a healthy diet, regular exercise, a comfortable, healthy environment, and through the use of medical advancements and vaccinations. All those nasty little bugs and diseases that our puppies used to pick up are now preventable.

If you haven't had a pet before, it can be daunting to find the right veterinarian. The best way to do it, in my experience, is by talking to other people who have dogs. They will be able to recommend the vets that they use and help you to avoid ones that they have bad experiences with.

Don't be afraid to change to a new veterinarian if you believe they are better suited for you and your dog. It's critical that you find a place and a person that your dog can feel comfortable and secure with. Remember, this is the person who is going to regularly use a rectal thermometer on your pooch. You best be sure that they like them!

Where Do I Start?

Pet insurance is a relatively new concept, and to non-pet owners, it sounds like a waste of money. For the first few months, it may seem so, but oh my word, when your dog gets sick, it is an absolute lifesaver! You can generally purchase different packages, much like our health insurance. Accidental plans, which cover any injuries, are as cheap as $4 a month, while some of the more expensive plans include vaccinations, dewormers, and grooming. Regardless of the plan you choose, I assure you, you won't regret it.

Microchipping and Identification

All dogs should be fitted with a collar and an identification tag. This may not seem so important, but if your dog were to go missing, you would regret not doing it. Your identification tag should consist of your dog's name and your mobile number. You don't need to put more information than that, other than perhaps a second number if you aren't great at keeping your phone on.

I highly recommend that you microchip your dog as well. These harmless, super tiny microchips are injected under your dog's skin. Each chip has a unique code, and local vets and shelters will have a scanner that they can use to ID your dog. The code is attached to your name, phone number, and email address, and they will be able to contact you if they find your pup.

Understanding Genetics

While unlikely in mixed-breed dogs, genetic disorders are sadly becoming more common in purebreds. Different breeds are susceptible to different disorders, so if you have a purebred dog with no background history, you will need to discuss the possibilities with your veterinarian. They will be able to assess your dog, identify any concerning symptoms, and inform you of any disorders that your breed may be prone to. If they do find something abnormal, they will conduct blood tests to detect any abnormal genes and give you an appropriate treatment plan that could prevent or stall the disorder.

Hip Dysplasia is one of the most common genetic disorders. It mainly affects larger breeds such as Labradors, German shepherds, and Great Danes. Hip Dysplasia occurs when puppies grow too quickly, and their weight places strain on their underdeveloped skeleton. This causes the hip joints to deform, which can become extremely painful. Surgery is the only way to fix this once it occurs.

Other disorders include Brachycephalic syndrome, which is a respiratory deformity that mainly impacts flat-faced breeds, and chondrodysplasia, which impacts long, short breeds such as bassets and dachshunds.

Medical Records

The first thing your veterinarian is going to ask you for is a medical history or breeder history. After this, your vet will ask you a couple of follow-up questions, such as: What do you feed them? How often do you exercise them, and what kind of environment do you live in?

You will need to be transparent, so don't try to hide anything. Veterinarians deal with all kinds of people each day, and some are too embarrassed to admit when they have made a mistake. Most people aren't as good at lying as they may think, and your vet will be able to see the truth when they examine your pup. If they don't, remember that you are compromising your dog's health and well-being. There is no shame in making an error, and each check-up should be treated as a learning experience for you.

You should keep all of your dog's medical records, vaccinations, and breeder certificates in a file. That way, if you do change veterinarians or if you have an emergency, you will be able to give them all the information they require.

The First Visit Is The Scariest

So, what actually happens after all the questions are completed?

First off, it's weighing time. That is, if you can actually get your dog onto their scale. Dogs act like scales are minefields, but then again, don't we all? Your puppies' weight is significant as it will impact their growth. These weights will be documented and referred to during the next check-up. This will provide an accurate growth chart and show you if your puppy is gaining or losing weight too quickly. If they are on the thin side, you may need to increase or change your food. However, if they are on the chunkier side, you may need to up your exercise time.

Your puppy will then be poked, prodded, and felt up and down to check for any abnormalities, dermatitis symptoms, and for fleas that may be using your pup as a bounce house. Eyes, ears, and mouth will be checked for any injuries, signs of illness, malnutrition, and dehydration.

The chances of anything being wrong with your puppy at this point are very low, so don't worry too much. Fecal floats are usually done routinely during check-ups. For this, your veterinarian will take a fecal sample using a pipette. This is just an all-around fun, family-friendly activity for both the pet and the owner. Sarcasm aside, it is essential, and once the sample is checked under a microscope, your vet will be able to identify any worms or eggs and treat your pup accordingly.

Important Pricks and Jabs

Once your dog has been treated or given a clean bill of health, it's vaccination time. These are less fun, and it's at this point that your dog may decide their vet is their new archenemy. Nevertheless, these vaccinations are incredibly important and can mean the difference between life and death in puppies.

What are They For?

Vaccinations are split into two categories. Mandatory and optional. Mandatory vaccinations may vary from state to state, and optional vaccinations are recommended based on your lifestyle.

Mandatory Vaccinations

DHPP, often referred to as 5 in 1—This cocktail protects your dog against distemper, parvovirus, parainfluenza, and 2 types of hepatitis.

Rabies—As the name suggests, the rabies vaccine is used to protect your dog against the rabies virus. Rabies is always fatal unless your dog is vaccinated or receives immediate treatment after they have come into contact with another rabid animal.

Common Optional Vaccinations

Lyme – If you and your pup enjoy hiking and if you live in an area that has a high Lyme disease rate, your veterinarian will likely recommend this vaccination.

Bordetella – The Bordetella vaccination is a must-have for puppies but is less common as your dog ages. This vaccination protects against kennel cough and is typically a non-negotiable vaccination for puppy schools, daycares, and boarding facilities.

Leptospirosis - This vaccination protects your dog against Leptospirosis bacteria, which is spread through urine and feces. While it isn't mandatory, your vet will recommend it if your dog is in frequent contact with wildlife and other dogs.

How Often Does My Dog Need To Endure This?

Your pup will receive four sets of vaccinations in the first year. The first is only given once your dog is fully weaned and 6–8 weeks old. Thereafter, they will be vaccinated at 10–12 weeks, 14–16 weeks, and 1 year of age. This is to build up enough immunity to effectively fight the potential illnesses. Once these vaccinations are complete, they will need to receive booster shots to maintain that immunity. These boosters are given every 1–2 years, depending on your lifestyle and your veterinarian's suggestion.

Getting Your Puppy Used to the Vet

Nobody likes going to the doctor, and we at least understand what they are telling us and doing to us. Imagine being a dog that suddenly lands up in a strange place with strange people that seem to smile at them yet proceed to violate them with thermometers!

To get them comfortable going to the vet, you should get them comfortable with getting in the car first. If they only get into the car to go to the vet, they will do the math and realize that a car ride is a one-way ticket to Injectionville. Take your puppy for regular car rides and get them used to stopping at random enjoyable places like a family or friend's house or a dog park.

When you get to the veterinarian's office, keep rewarding them for any good behavior. If they walk through the door nicely, treat. If they sit well in the waiting room, treat!

The moment you walk into the consulting room, your veterinarian will do the same thing to create a happy association with your dog. Reassuring your dog and rewarding them through procedures is vital, and it's important to leave on a happy note so that they are not scared to go back. I am a big sucker, and after every vet visit, my dog walks out with a new toy.

When Should I Panic?

Every little sneeze or stumble can send you into a panic when you get your first puppy. I remember staying up and watching my little one breathe. Counting how many seconds between each breath and spiraling into dismay if it varied too much. It was a little crazy, but that's love for you!

The good news is while your puppy's immune system isn't quite up to scratch just yet, it is actually pretty easy to keep them alive.

Creepy Crawlies

Ugh, these are gross. If your pup spends a lot of time outdoors or has frequent contact with other dogs, it is likely that they are going to pick up some parasites.

Worms

Worms are usually picked up from contaminated soil, rotten foods, and feces; as we all know, and if you don't, get prepared! Dogs love eating cat poop and in fact, rolling in any poop that didn't come from another dog. It is absolutely disgusting and often makes us question why on earth we decided to adopt such foul beasts. Yet, we still bathe them off while holding our noses and trying not to throw up.

This kind of behavior makes it easy for the nasty little worms to infect them. The most common worms include hookworm, roundworm, heartworm, tapeworm, and whipworm. The first sign of a worm invasion is an increase in appetite and scooting. Scooting is when your pup places their butt on the floor and drags themselves along it to cure the itch. Carpets seem to be the favorite scooting arena, with the white ones being first prize. If left untreated, your pup will start to lose weight and develop diarrhea, and you may find blood or worms in their poop.

Thankfully, this is easily treatable and preventable. Doggy dewormers are a must, and it's recommended that they are given every three months to prevent infection.

Ticks, Fleas, and Mites

Fleas are extremely itchy and irritating, and you will find your dog scratching themselves uncontrollably. You may even see the fleas jumping off your dog's skin. These are not really life-threatening, but that doesn't mean that you shouldn't treat your dog for them immediately. They can infest your house, and if your dog continuously scratches, they can create wounds.

Honestly, there's not much that can freak me out as much as a disgusting fat tick. These sneaky little bugs that burrow into your dog's skin. These are a little more difficult to see, especially in long-haired dogs, but regular brushing and strokes will help you to check for them. If you find a tick, you will need to pull it off and pop it (eww!) immediately. One or two ticks are generally not a problem but depending on where you live, some ticks carry Lyme disease. You will need to monitor your dog carefully for any symptoms and check yourself for any ticks.

If you notice that your dog is constantly itchy, yet there are no signs of fleas, they probably have mites. These are microscopic and, if left untreated, can cause mange, which is highly infectious and contagious to other animals. If you take your dog for hikes or regular walks through forests and tall grass, it's best to medicate them throughout the year.

Chewable parasite medications are available, and these will kill off any ticks, fleas, and mites and prevent them from attaching to your dog. These last one to three months, depending on the brand you purchase. Some of them contain a dewormer, making it easy to treat your dog for everything all in one go.

Kennel Cough and Sniffles

Bordetella, or kennel cough, is a nasty and incredibly contagious virus. It's called kennel cough because it is one of the most commonly spread viruses in boarding and rescue facilities. The most common symptom is a cough or hack. It becomes more severe when your dog exercises. In healthy adult dogs, this cough is usually nothing more than an irritation that goes away with a few days of rest.

However, in young or senior dogs that are immunocompromised, it can cause some serious damage to the heart and lungs. If your puppy is coughing while resting, you will need to isolate them from any other pets in the household. It's best to take them to the vet for treatment, as you don't want to risk it turning into pneumonia.

Belly Aches

Be prepared to deal with quite a few stomach issues. Puppies aren't the smartest when it comes to eating weird things, and it can take them a while to figure out what is good and what is bad.

Diarrhea

Diarrhea is usually caused by eating food that doesn't quite agree with their stomach, but it could also indicate that your pup has worms and, in severe cases, parvovirus. Parvovirus is deadly, and it is mandatory to vaccinate your dog against it. It is highly contagious and spreads quickly. If you notice worms, blood, or slime in their poo, it's time to panic.

Vomiting

Vomiting is often due to overeating or, again, eating things they shouldn't. My pup once threw up the pieces of an entire Tupperware lid. Why would he eat that? I have no clue, but he is a dog, and that's what dogs do! It's best to check if there are any foreign objects or blood in the vomit and contact your vet if you are worried they have eaten something toxic.

Constipation

It is a bit more difficult to find the cause of constipation. Overeating can cause it, as their little bodies aren't able to process huge amounts of food in one go or even in one day. Blockages from eating weird objects are also a possibility. If you suspect this, you need to get emergency assistance, as it could become life-threatening. The other possibility is that your puppy is simply holding it in too long. You need to give them regular potty breaks and keep up the exercise.

For all stomach upsets, it's best to stop feeding them for 12 to 24 hours. Give them electrolytes and probiotics, which will help keep them hydrated and restore the healthy bacteria in their stomach. The rule of thumb is if it happens once or twice, you don't need to worry. However, if it continues over 24 hours, it is time to panic!

Puppies Sure Do Love Mud

Oh boy; they do indeed. I am yet to see a puppy that can resist rolling in sand, mud, or worse. This is not only fun for them, but it is also a way for them to groom themselves and scratch that itch they can't reach. It's just unfortunate for us, as we aren't too keen on muddy paws on the clean floor or a wet, dirty body sleeping on the couch.

What You Need

First things first. You will need to get equipped. Nail clippers are the most common and easiest tool to use for nail grooming. However, nail grinders are a good choice for large dogs with extremely thick nails.

Buy a good sensitive skin, natural shampoo. Regardless of whether your puppy suffers from a condition or not. They will inevitably drink the water they are bathing in and lick themselves dry. You really don't want them to be ingesting chemicals!

A good brush, depending on your dog's hair type, and I suggest you get a water brush as well to use during bath time. If you have a breed that is going to need regular haircuts, you can look into buying pet clippers. These are expensive, though, and you may want to stick with the groomers for now.

A doggy toothbrush and natural dog toothpaste are a must. This may not seem important now, but you will regret not doing it when your dog enters their senior years and has to get a number of their teeth extracted.

Scrub a Dub Dub

Give your dog a good brushing before you get to the bath. This will untangle any knots, remove the excess fur and loosen up any dirt on their skin or hair. Using lukewarm water, fill your bathtub or dish tub up to around your dog's knees. You want them to be able to comfortably sit down and not feel the need to swim.

Lather them up with a natural puppy shampoo and use your water brush to really get under their fur. Make sure that you wash their bellies and armpits well. Once you're done, rinse them off thoroughly. Empty the dirty water and rinse your dog's legs off again to make sure there is no shampoo lingering. Don't wash their faces unless you are using a tear-free puppy shampoo, and even then, be careful. You want to avoid getting water or shampoo in their ears, eyes, mouth, and nose. Once the bath is done, dry them off. It's best to get your dog used to a hair dryer early, especially if they will be going to the groomers, where it will be used regularly. Put it on the lowest setting and on the lowest heat so that it is not too overpowering. Again, avoid their faces.

Whether you use a towel or a hair dryer, it's good to ensure that their bellies and armpits are completely dry. This is where your puppy stores its heat, and if that area is wet and cold, you are putting them at risk. Their bodies should be dry enough that when they do give a little shake, no water sprays you.

Let's See That Pretty Face

Once their bath is complete, use a damp, warm cotton cloth or similar and wipe their faces clean. You will need to do this a few times to ensure that you actually get all the dirt off. You can gently clean their eyes with a cotton pad if that is easier. For their ears, dab a cotton pad into baby oil and gently clean around the underside of the ear. You don't want to go too deep, and you don't want any oil going into the ear canal, as this can cause infection.

A good bath and face cleaning should be done around twice a month. If you have a pigsty puppy, then move it up to weekly. Bathing is not natural for them, and their skin secretes special oils which keep their fur waterproof. Bathing them too often can damage the skin and reduce the oil production, leading to dermatitis. This is another reason why buying a natural shampoo is best, as there are no harsh chemicals to damage their skin and glands.

Lastly, it's time to brush their teeth. Be gentle, and don't force your pup into it. You want this to be a fun experience, and you should reward them during each step. First, just place the toothbrush near their mouths. If they aren't worried, reward them. Then you can put it into their mouths. Reward them if they are good. You can then brush the front teeth and work your way to the back. Go in gentle, circular motions and make each session as short as possible. You probably won't be able to get in and brush their teeth completely on the first try, and that's cool. You have time. I like to brush my dog's teeth every second day for just a few minutes at a time.

Mani-Pedi

This is likely the hardest grooming step to get your dog used to. Ever try to hold down an Irish wolfhound for a nail clipping? That's not the kind of nightmare you want to deal with later in life!

Hold your puppy still in a sitting position. Lift their front paw up and backward so that it is comfortable, then reward them when they sit still. Put the clippers over the nail and reward them when they are calm.

Next, clip the nail. This is when your pooch is going to get a fright. That noise is quite intense and unexpected. Give them a break and a ton of treats, and then repeat the steps above.

It's unlikely that you will need to clip your dog's nails when they are a puppy. Running on hard surfaces and asphalt will file the nails down naturally. Even so, it's best to practice getting your puppy in that position and the sound of the clippers, even if you don't actually cut a nail. You will need to get them into a standing position to work on the hind nails. However, if you are just practicing, work on getting the position for the front paws perfected first.

A full grooming session may be a bit too much for a young puppy to sit through. Try to split up the steps throughout the month.

Chapter 5:

Relationships Are Built on Treats

Is puppy-specific food really worth it? Yes, yes, it is. Dogs, just like people, have specific dietary requirements that need to be met as they go through each life stage. Think of it this way, feeding a baby a cheeseburger is probably not the best way to facilitate healthy growth. Luckily, some brilliant people out there have made our jobs easy and formulated specialized diets that keep our dogs healthy during each of these stages.

For the first year or two, your puppy is growing. Rapidly! They also expend a huge amount of energy, which means they require some pretty vital nutrients and proteins to facilitate this. Once they are fully grown, they will need to be fed a diet that can maintain their bodies' health while still providing them with enough energy for moderate exercise.

Once they hit their senior years, they are unlikely to be less active, and a lot of the ingredients in puppy and adult food can lead to some serious weight gain. Senior dogs will develop a number of age-related medical conditions, and a senior diet will contain vitamins and minerals that will ease these aches and pains.

Let's Get Chewing

As daunting as the dog food aisle may be; you only need to risk it once or, to be fair, once for each life stage. For the first year or two of your dog's life, you will need high-quality puppy food. Thereafter, you can move on to an adult diet and swap to a senior one when your dog hits seven years. I, personally, like to use the same brand throughout my pup's life because why fix something that isn't broken? Constantly swapping brands will mess with your dog's digestive system, and you can expect some nasty results.

Vital Ingredients

Let's not jump down the rabbit hole of dog nutrition. This is a complicated science that is best left up to the professionals. All we need to know is the most important ingredients to look for.

Protein content and amino acids are arguably the most important ingredients to look for when choosing food. According to Dr. Ochoa, puppies require a 22-32% protein content. To put this in perspective, adult dog food has an average of 18% (Lauren, 2022). This, along with a higher amount of calcium and phosphorus, is required to build and support healthy bones and muscles.

While adult and senior foods try to stick to a lower fat and carbohydrate content, puppy food should be loaded with it. This is because puppies expend an abnormal amount of energy. I swear, they can actually walk up walls when they get excited enough. Dr. Williams and Dr. Downing found that a diet with 10-20% fat content and 20%

or more carbohydrate content is recommended to meet your puppy's needs (Williams & Downing, n.d.).

Size and Breed Matters

The majority of dog food brands will sell their kibble in three different sizes, small, medium, or large, to better suit your breed. If you have a mini breed, it's probably best not to give them kibble the size of their paws, as these can damage their teeth.

If you have a highly specialized breed, you should purchase breed-specific food. These are specially formulated for your dog and contain minerals, vitamins, and ingredients that are best suited to the breed.

Most breed-specific foods cater to small and mini dogs such as Pomeranians, pugs, and Yorkshire terriers. However, you can now purchase food designed for Labradors, Great Danes, and German shepherds, which specifically supports bone growth and joint health.

If you are unsure what to buy your pup, ask your vet or your breeder. They will be able to recommend some good ones.

Kibbles and Cans

Dry food is the most popular option for pet owners. It is easy to store, doesn't go bad quickly, and it's a breeze to measure out and feed in the morning. They contain all the protein, minerals, and fat that your pup needs to grow and remain healthy. Dry food is also great for your dog's teeth, and each time your pup chews, the rough pieces will dislodge any plaque that may have built up. However, this food can become a bit boring, and it is always nice to switch things up a little.

Canned food is definitely tastier, and if given the chance, your dog will choose it every time. The soft chunks and gravies are fantastic for easy eating and digestion, making it a great option for dogs recovering from illness or injury. If you intend to feed your dog canned food, you will need to brush their teeth more regularly to keep them clean.

While canned foods can be just as healthy as dry foods, it's important to do your research before you commit to them full-time. The cheaper canned foods work well as a treat or to use on top of dry food as a gravy, but they are full of fats and carbohydrates. Feeding your pup these cans cause several stomach issues and turn them into furry barrels of fat.

Vet-approved canned foods are a much better option, although quite a bit pricier. They are formulated for full-time use and contain the necessary ingredients your dog needs to thrive.

How Much Is Too Much?

Each bag of food will come with a recommended feeding chart. This chart will tell you how many ounces your puppy should be fed each day depending on their current weight. More expensive and specialized foods will have three columns and will recommend how much food your puppy should get based on their activity level.

A low-energy puppy that wouldn't be able to burn off the food as quickly may get 5 ounces a day, while a high-energy puppy will get 7 ounces a day. The amount per day should then be split up equally into the number of feeds you give them.

These measurements are incredibly important, especially during their growing years. They are especially vital for large and giant breeds that are prone to hip dysplasia, as it ensures they grow at a normal pace.

This also means that you are going to need to get a scale. Don't worry, you don't have to weigh your pup every day, but I do suggest you do it once a week so that you can increase their food regularly. Once their weight begins to stabilize, you should weigh them every one to three months.

Supplements

If you are feeding your pooch high-quality puppy food, you probably won't need to give them any supplements at all. That being said, there are some nice ones that are worth having on hand for when they are feeling a little under the weather.

A good stock of probiotics is in order. This powdered supplement can be sprinkled over food or mixed into water. It helps to keep your pup's stomach working correctly and is especially useful if they are recovering from an illness or injury. If you have a dumpster-diving puppy, you may want to use these more regularly.

Mobility supplements that contain glucosamine and antioxidants are a great supplement for large and giant breeds that are prone to hip dysplasia and arthritis. The glucosamine will help keep their joints healthy and in good working order, while the antioxidants will keep inflammation and swelling down. It's best to use these supplements throughout your dog's life to get the best results.

Omega oil supplements promote healthy skin and fur. This is a wonderful supplement to give to puppies that suffer from skin conditions, ticks, and fleas.

Immune system and antioxidant supporters should be used for puppies that are recovering from any medical issues. These boost the immune system and work at easing any inflammation and pain.

All puppy foods are rich in calcium, but occasionally, your vet may recommend that you give them an additional supplement. This is usually the case for very young puppies that are still being bottle-fed or for puppies that have had any issues with their bone growth.

You can never go wrong with a good multivitamin! These promote overall good health and can be used throughout your dog's life.

You can buy gummy or chewy health supplements, although they may be a bit more expensive. It is worth it, though, especially if you have a pup that can smell medication from a mile away.

Be careful not to mix too many supplements together, as they can have negative effects.

Treats

I wasn't kidding when I said relationships are based on treats. Whether you're training your dog, you want their attention, or you just want to buy their love, give them a treat. However, a treat should be used as a treat. Continuously giving your pup treats will take away their significance, and your dog is unlikely to be as excited or motivated when they get one. Never mind the weight they will gain!

Make sure that you don't let them manipulate you with their big puppy eyes for more. However, let's be honest here, who can actually resist them? For this reason, it's a good idea to invest in a variety of treats.

Training Treats

During training, you will be giving your dog plenty of treats. Seriously, you will be going through them like tic tacs. When choosing your training treats, you will need to find ones low in fat and sugar. Dogs prefer quantity over quality during training, so try to get the smallest ones available.

I personally like to have two or three types of flavors on hand during training. I switch to a different treat type when I notice that my dog is getting bored or when they do something superb and deserve a big reward.

Tasty Treats

Sometimes dogs deserve treats for no other reason than existing. This kind of sweet reward is great to build up your relationship and keep them busy. These need to be high-quality, absolutely irresistible treats. Large, chewable treats or peanut butter is a great way to keep your dog stimulated during their downtime. I won't lie; I like to use low-fat peanut butter because it ends up entertaining both of us. That chewing face is just too funny. If you just want to build up your relationship, smaller treats work well as you can give more of them.

Dental Treats

These are my favorite. They are large chewy treats that contain several natural ingredients that help clean your dog's teeth. They are made in such a way that your dog will have to chew on them for a good few minutes to get through. Keeping them entertained at the same time.

Liver Bread

If you are worried about what goes into store-bought treats, I have the solution for you. You can make your own! Liver bread is pretty disgusting, and I can't imagine eating it myself, but dogs go absolutely mad for it. It's easy to make, and you can bake large batches at a time and freeze them for later use.

Ingredients

1. 500g Raw liver

2. 3 Eggs

3. 1 Cup flour

4. **1 ⅓ Cup whole-wheat flour**

5. 1 Teaspoon baking powder

6. Onion, beef, or chicken seasoning or stock cubes (optional)

7. Grated raw butternut, baby marrow, broccoli, or pumpkin (optional)

Method

1. Blend the eggs and raw liver together

2. Mix the blended mixture with the dry ingredients

3. Add in vegetables and seasoning

4. Place mixture into a large flat baking tray

5. Bake at 356° F for 15 minutes

6. Allow to cool and cut into squares

7. Bribe your dog into doing whatever you want them to do!

If you are worried about any of the ingredients, swap them out! If you are worried about the flour, you can change to a gluten-free or rice flour option.

Mom Says Chocolate Isn't Good for Dogs

Ever dealt with the consequences of a dog stealing some cake? Trust me. You never ever want to. It involves plenty of paper towels, boiling water, and an air freshener. It's not just chocolate, either. Dogs LOVE food and will take a slice of anything that is left out.

Absolute No, No's	Toxic but Not Deadly in Small Doses	Not Toxic but Certainly Not Good
Alcohol	Avocado	Milk and Dairy
Chocolate and Coffee	Citrus	Raw Meat
Grapes and Raisins	Coconut	Raw Eggs
Macadamia Nuts	Onions and Garlic	Yeast

Absolute No, No's	Toxic but Not Deadly in Small Doses	Not Toxic but Certainly Not Good
Xylitol	Salty Food and Snacks	Uncooked Bones

These are just a few of the most harmful foods your dog may get into. In fact, there aren't actually many human foods that are safe for dogs to eat. While the first little bite won't harm them, continuous access can cause immense weight gain and upset stomachs.

Every time I hear an owner say, "Well, I give them the leftovers that have been in the fridge for a while, I would rather not waste food!" I could pull my own and their hair out. Your dog is not your trash can, and this can cause severe, sometimes fatal consequences.

Helpful Tools

Mealtime doesn't have to be a hassle, and there are several tools that make preparation and feeding quick, easy, and much more enjoyable.

Food and Water Bowls

Don't limit yourself to one of each. Otherwise, you will be constantly moving them around the house. I suggest buying a nice big water bowl for outdoors, a smaller one for their play area, and one to go with their food bowl. Stainless-steel dishes are your best bet. They are much more hygienic, durable, and can easily be washed in the dishwasher. But they can get hot in the sun, and dogs aren't particularly fond of tea, so make sure the water is in the shade.

When picking out a food bowl, make sure that you get something suitable for your dog's size. A large dog bowl is not going to work for small breeds, and they will spend half their time searching for their food. For giant breeds, I recommend that you get a bowl stand, which lifts the bowls off the floor and brings them closer to your dog's height. Constantly leaning down to eat can put pressure on your dog's neck and joints, which can be uncomfortable and potentially cause issues in their later years.

Food bowls should be cleaned after every meal, and water bowls should be rinsed and refilled at least once a day to reduce algae and bacteria buildup.

Slow Feeders

If your dog is a glutton, it's time to get a slow feeder. Puppies that suck up their food like vacuum cleaners can become bloated and, in some cases, throw up their food. They are less likely to actually chew their kibble, which can cause constipation.

These bowls have bumps and ridges inside of them, which makes your pup work a little harder for their food, and it gives their stomach time to register that it is full. You can go one step further and buy an interactive feeding bowl. I love these as they make dinnertime fun.

Lick Mats

Lick mats are a super fun enrichment tool that is great for dogs of all ages. These silicon mats have various textures, which makes it difficult to lick the food off. It also just feels great to lick them; you should try it sometime. Layering soft canned foods and treats such as peanut butter on them is sure to keep your dog entertained for a while.

Scale, Measuring Scoops, and Cups

Depending on the dog food you buy, you may get a measuring cup. These have gram or ounce measurements on the side, which help you to easily measure out your dog's food. Just remember that these cups are food-specific. Larger or smaller kibble of another brand will weigh more or less than the cup indicates. I prefer to weigh my food in a transparent cup on a scale. When I have the right amount, I mark it with a line and my dog's name. Since I have a multi-dog household, I use the same cup and mark off each dog's food amount. This makes dishing up meals so much easier!

Food Bin

Many brands have started fitting their dog foods with reusable seals to keep the food fresh between uses. I don't really trust these, and I find that they constantly snap open by themselves, and large bags of food for big breeds don't have them equipped. An airtight food bin is best. It stops spilling unwanted creepy crawlies, and honestly, it just looks better. My neat freak brain is in love with the fact that I don't have to have the food bags sprawled around the kitchen. Instead, I have three food bins stacked next to each other, with my dog's bowls and measuring cups on top.

Chapter 6:

Smiles, Not Snarls!

Dogs are (mostly) highly social creatures and have never quite shaken off the pack mentally of their ancestors. Even though you have now become a part of their pack family, it's not quite the same as having another furry friend who doesn't mind being chased around and jumped on. Puppies are still getting used to not having their littermates around, and the lack of constant canine attention makes them extra eager to make new friends and enjoy some dog-on-dog playtime.

Sometimes, a little too eager. While you would think it would be easy to socialize a puppy, you need to consider your dog's social intelligence and the personality of their new playmate. Puppies that are taken away from their mom and littermates too early don't quite learn how to speak dog and can be overly clinging, which annoys their playmates. Especially older dogs that don't have much patience. Because of this, it's important to learn how to safely introduce your bundle of joy to other dogs and keep them from having negative experiences that may cause fear and aggression later in life.

Learning to Speak Dog

So, you have already learned a little bit about puppy body language and how they communicate with us. Now it is time to learn a bit more about how they communicate with each other. These signs and signals are vital during socialization attempts, as they will allow you to avoid potentially dangerous situations and fights.

Positive Body Language

Positive body language indicates that your pup is relaxed, happy, or excited. Their entire demeanor should look loose. Muscles relaxed, ears flopping around, and their tail should be hanging or wagging in long slow movements.

When excited, that tail speeds up, and their whole body begins to wag with it. They may even seem like they have a smile on their face! If they are bouncing from wall to wall and bowing down with their butts in the air, they are feeling extra playful.

A relaxed puppy stays loose but is happy to relax on a bed or in the sun. They are still confident in themselves and will hold their heads high when they aren't lying down. Their ears may perk up now and again if something interesting happens around them, but they aren't too worried about getting involved.

Negative Body Language

Negative body language indicates that your puppy is either scared, aggressive, or overly dominant. Their bodies are noticeably tense, and you can see their muscles through the fur. Aggressive and dominant dogs will stand tall and still with their ears erect. Their tails will stand upright and sometimes wag in rapid, short motions, which indicates arousal. You will notice that they are fixated on a target and won't take their eyes off it unless you drag them away.

Depending on the situation, they may start to produce a low growl and bend down slightly as if to stalk prey.

A scared dog, on the other hand, will try to make itself as small as possible so that it is less of a target. They will hold their tail between their legs and cower. Their ears will be flat against their head, and they try their best to avoid eye contact with whatever is terrifying them. If the situation becomes too intense, they may whimper or cry out before running away.

Excitable behavior can often turn into dominant behavior quickly if you aren't monitoring them. The more hyped up they get, the more boisterous the play becomes, and in due time, somebody is going to become frustrated and nip. The adrenaline coursing through their veins from the excitement can turn to dominance or aggression.

If your puppies are roughhousing and getting a little too excitable, call them back to you and give them a second to refocus and relax before letting them play again.

Socialization Goals

First, figure out what your actual socialization goals are, and train your dog according to them. Going too far in your training can cause you and your pup unnecessary stress. Remember, puppies are just as good at forgetting as they are learning. So, whatever your goal is, you will need to stay consistent.

Introverts and Extroverts

Some dogs are the ultimate extroverts. They will bound up to any stranger or dog and give them a big sloppy kiss hello. They just love attention and snuggles! This behavior is fantastic and will give you a head start in training. However, that doesn't mean that no training is required. Such behavior can be viewed as bad manners, and if you don't teach your dog recall, you are in for trouble. Not everyone wants to be greeted that way, especially reactive or nervous dogs. Children especially can be knocked over like bowling pins if your dog is on the larger side.

On the other hand, you get introverts. These aren't as rare as you may think. No matter how much you try to socialize them, they simply aren't interested in the company of others and prefer to keep you all to themselves. This is okay. The important thing is to ensure that you train them well enough to not fear or react negatively during social situations.

Family Comes First

A family-friendly dog is easy enough to raise, especially if you already have a partner and children. Children that treat a dog well will be treated back with respect. If your dog is less friendly to your child, you should investigate the situation further, as they may be making some serious pet care mistakes.

If you do not have children but plan to one day, or if you plan to take your pup with you to family events, you will need to get your dog used to being played with. Believe it or not, some dogs are petrified of children. Who can blame them? They terrify me, too, sometimes. Dogs can't quite understand why they are so small yet so loud. They almost seem to be the same as them, but they have no tails or fur. It can be difficult for them to adjust to that kind of attention.

In this case, the only option is to have regular little visitors so that your pup can get a chance to interact with them and learn their ways. Be sure to reward them for good behavior and remove them or the child from the situation if your pup becomes a little too hyped up. It's best to give them both a short rest to calm down.

A Confident Walker

This is a non-negotiable goal, especially if you are planning to walk your dog. A confident and happy dog will be able to casually walk down the street with you with no fuss at all. Even if they are not quite a social butterfly, you don't want them to react negatively to any strangers or strange dogs. It can become pretty embarrassing when you walk out the gate only for them to bark at the neighbors and passing cars.

What Could Go Wrong?

Safety is a priority. This goes for you, your dog, and those around them. If you find that your dog is becoming more reactive with every walk, it's time to put a halt to the whole operation and go back to the basics. An aggressive encounter is the quickest way to create a reactive and fearful puppy. It can be difficult to bring them back from this point, but there are some foolproof solutions if you are consistent enough in your training.

No dog is inherently aggressive, and they don't take pleasure in the act. When your dog reaches their threshold, they have two options. Fight or flight. If they can't flee, they are going to try their hardest to scare the living daylights out of whatever is triggering them.

Working through this fear before you get back to walking is vital. If this is something that you are struggling with, don't worry. I will be covering the solution in Chapter 10.

Puppy Illness

Puppy daycares, regular walks, and any interactions which involve other dogs can invite some unwanted illnesses. This is why vaccinations exist!

Even if the dogs around you are not protected from these illnesses, you can ensure that yours is. Illness is not the only thing to worry about. If your pup enjoys sniffing poop or other dogs' butts, they can become vulnerable to parasitic infections. Again, this can be controlled, and as a responsible pet owner, you should be taking all the preventive steps you can.

Say Hello to My Little Friend

Introducing your puppy to humans is effortless. Your pup is open to new and exciting things, and they have already figured out that you were worth the effort; why not everyone else?!

The only problem with human introductions is the humans. You will need to be confident and speak for your puppy before somebody else gets to touch him. Let them know what they are allowed and not allowed to do. Immediately picking them up and swinging them around is a definite no, no. Roughhousing and play fighting with them is a no, no! Children, especially, struggle to understand how to meet a dog, and many will go straight in for a tackle or a shout.

Any over-excitable or potentially scary experience like this can affect your dog in the long term. They can develop associations of fear with the person who scared or hurt them, and this not only affects that relationship but many others.

You may find that they suddenly have an issue with meeting men, people with blonde hair, or people that wear hats. It seems strange at first until you remember that a man with blonde hair that was wearing a hat gave them a smack when they were younger.

Calm and collected introductions are the only way forward. Allow the stranger to kneel to their level, pat them gently and speak to them in a calming voice. Add in a few treats for luck, and your pup will have a new best friend in no time.

Dog Introductions

Very young puppies don't seem to have any issue meeting and making new friends. They are still in littermate mode and will readily jump on the first fluff ball they find. However, your puppy is going through their learning phases, and it's difficult to socialize them when they go through their cautious, fearful stage. Try to get them used to new puppies before this, as it will allow them to learn good doggy etiquette.

Important Considerations

It might not be the best option to introduce a tiny toy puppy to a larger, boisterous one. Large dogs don't really know their size, and as puppies, they are clumsy and playful and may just trample your pooch into the ground like a tent peg. It is not impossible to introduce them; you will just need to monitor them carefully.

Age gaps and temperaments also need to be considered. While most adult dogs are more accepting of a puppy over another adult, puppies can be quite annoying. If the dog you are introducing them to has a short fuse, your pup may end up having a bad experience. Do not introduce your puppy to a known reactive dog at this point!

Puppy Parties

Dog parks can be incredibly overwhelming for an under-socialized puppy, and you will need to proceed with caution if you notice that they feel uncomfortable. Imagine throwing an introvert on stage in front of hundreds of people! The standard response is panic, babbling, and then sprinting away. That's precisely what your pooch will do, although the babble may turn into a bite. Only go to the dog park when you are sure they are ready.

Obedience school is a fantastic way for them to socialize, as all the pups in the class will be focused on their owners and training. This breaks the ice a little, as they can become comfortable in each other's presence before meeting properly. However, obedience school is open to a lot of less knowledgeable pet owners, and you will need to stand your ground if they cross boundaries. Some owners may find it perfectly acceptable to let their dog run off leash and straight into your dog's mouth!

Puppy daycare is another great way to socialize your puppy. It's best to start them off at a young age and ensure that the daycare only has dogs that are of similar age. The best part of using a daycare is the staff. They are trained in caring for dogs and are always available to monitor the puppy party.

The Right Way to Introduce

As your pup gets older, you will need to take some extra steps when introducing them to a new friend. You should ALWAYS introduce dogs on mutual ground. Using one dog's territory will automatically create a bit of tension, which you don't want. Set up a puppy play date with a friend and organize to meet them at a park or a quiet lot.

1. Stand a couple of meters away from each other. Far enough that your dogs can't approach each other but close enough that they can see and smell each other.

2. Keep your dog's focus on you by playing a game or practicing some tricks.

3. Once they are calm, you can begin clicking and treating them every time they look over at the other dog. This will create a positive association with the other dog. Be careful not to reward them if they are displaying any negative behaviors.

4. Start to walk a bit closer and chat with your friend. Your confident, calm and happy state will become contagious, and your pup will be more intrigued than worried.

5. Keep rewarding them whenever they are relaxed or sitting obediently.

6. Once you're close enough, allow the two dogs to give each other a good sniff and then walk away. Don't let this interaction go over two to three minutes.

7. Distract your dog again by playing some fun games!

8. Repeat the steps until your dogs are comfortable with each other.

9. If you notice that either of them are becoming distressed by the situation, call it quits for the day and try again another time.

If your dog doesn't like another dog, it doesn't mean that they are unfriendly or aggressive. Just like us, they have preferences, and it's not their fault if they don't find the other dog funny or smart.

Chapter 7:

Training A, B, C's

A is for apple, b is for BALL!, c is for CAT!, and d is for DOOR! Thankfully, your dog doesn't need to learn the alphabet except for a few of the most important words. One of which starts with a T! Treat is probably the most dangerous word your dog could ever learn. Once they make the association, there is no stopping them from doing what it takes to get the reward. While this is remarkable in training sessions, it's less so when you are on the phone with a friend and find yourself saying. "Let's go out tonight, it's my t-r-e-a-t." It's easier to spell it out than deal with the fallout of your dog's tantrum.

Okay, enough jokes. Let's get serious. Puppies do need training, and the behaviors you will be teaching them are a lot more than neat little "tricks." These are foundational commands that are used to teach your dog basic manners. Without them, you won't be able to untrain negative behaviors such as jumping or proceeding to more advanced training. There are tons of ways to train a dog, but there are only a few ways to get the training to actually stick. Let's get to it…

Pawsitive Parenting

Positive reinforcement is the most popular method of training, and most trainers and behaviorists will recommend it over others. It forms one part of the four quadrants of training, and you will need to have a good understanding of each to make the right calls. Learning each section can be a little tricky at first; the names, in particular, can make things confusing.

The Four Quadrants

In this context, positive refers to adding or including a stimulus or item. Negative refers to subtracting a stimulus or item. Reinforcement refers to motivating your dog to keep displaying the behavior, while punishment refers to stopping your dog from displaying a behavior.

Positive Reinforcement

Positive reinforcement is easy. This involves rewarding your dog with a stimulus when they display a positive behavior. By rewarding this kind of behavior, your dog is more likely to repeat it, as they have developed a positive association with it.

Example: Giving your dog a treat when they walk calmly next to you.

Negative Reinforcement

By removing an item or stimulus, you can increase your chances of your dog displaying a behavior. Confused yet? Let's put it in a more understandable example.

Your dog likes to pull on the leash, so you decide to put a choke collar (stimulus) on him. When he pulls, he gets choked, but when he stops pulling, he is rewarded (stimulus removed) by not being in pain or discomfort. This makes it more likely for him to walk without pulling.

Positive Punishment

Positive punishment involves adding in a stimulus to stop your dog from displaying a behavior. The added stimulus is generally something painful or scary. Sadly, too many of us use this method when we are frustrated.

Example: You tug back forcefully when your dog pulls on the leash. Others include hitting them when they bark or shouting at them when they chew on something.

Negative Punishment

This involves subtracting a stimulus or reward to stop your dog from displaying a behavior.

Example: Your dog is pulling on the leash, so you stop walking. You have taken away the reward of them going for a walk. Once they display good behavior or stand calmly next to you, you reward them by continuing the walk.

Negative reinforcement and positive punishment are sadly still used in the training world, but it has become less common. While these methods may produce immediate results, they come with side effects, and most dogs that are trained through this are found to be more fearful, less obedient, and less likely to be interested in learning new things.

Positive reinforcement and negative punishment are, however, two methods that can and should be used throughout your training journey.

Clicker Training

During positive reinforcement training, the goal is to reward your dog at the exact moment they display good behavior. However, that is a little difficult if they are on the other side of the room. By delaying giving them the treat, your dog may be unsure of which behavior they are actually being rewarded for. Was it for sitting? Standing up? Or walking toward you? This is where bridging or marking comes in.

It's pretty simple. The dog does something good, you bridge (confirm) the behavior, and then you treat them. Bridging is usually vocal, and the word "good!" is commonly used.

Clicker training makes this much easier. The small handheld device will make a clicking noise when you press it, and this noise is used to mark or bridge the exact moment that your dog displays a good behavior, which means you never miss a beat.

In order to use clicker training, you first need to get your dog used to the clicker and what it means. All you need to do is get their attention, click, and then treat them. Continue doing this until they associate the click with a treat, but make sure they are focusing on you when you click so that you don't accidentally reward a different behavior.

Training Tools

You don't really need much more than a bag of healthy treats to begin training your pup. However, if you would like to go a step further, there are some helpful tools that make your experience easier.

Rewards

Rewards shouldn't just be treats. These may seem like the most obvious and tastiest option, but some dogs actually prefer to receive a toy as a reward! Incorporating a toy into your routine will also help stop your dog from putting on all those extra calories. A tug rope or fluffy toy is usually the best for training as these are interactive and keep their focus on you.

Treat Bag

Scratch what I said earlier. A treat bag is an absolute necessity. There is nothing worse than having loose, damp treats falling out of your pocket or having your dog tackle you down for the bundle you are trying to hold in your hand. A treat bag is waterproof, clips onto your belt or purse, and has a drawstring that makes it easy to open or close.

Yoga Mat

I like to use a yoga mat during training, especially if I am teaching my dog behaviors that require them to sit or lay on the floor. Hardwood floors, tiles, asphalt, and concrete are all very uncomfortable and can hurt your pup's paws and elbows if you ask them to lean on them too long.

Patience

The most important tool in your arsenal. Take a couple of deep breaths and get yourself into the right mindset before you start training. Don't bring bad energy into a happy space. If you feel frustrated, scrap the training for the day.

Thinking Caps On!

This is probably one of the cutest parts of owning a puppy. Seeing that tail wag and their minds working overtime to figure out what you want from them. They are trying so hard, and when that little lightbulb goes off and they succeed, their joy could just make you cry. Your happiness and excitement are contagious, and if you treat their success like a big deal, they will too.

You want to constantly make training a fun and exciting experience. If your pup gets tired or bored, stop it there and give them a break. If they struggle to master a new behavior, they switch back to an old one they have already mastered to build their confidence up. Set them up to succeed by training them in a quiet space with no distractions. The moment their minds wander, your training becomes ten times more difficult.

Below are the six most important behaviors that every pup should master!

Sit

The absolute bare minimum behavior that your dog should know. It's generally used as a calming and refocus cue. If your pup's butt is on the floor, they can't jump on you! If they are sitting, they are more likely to focus their full attention on you. Until your dog knows how to sit on cue, you cannot advance to training new behaviors.

1. Get their focus on you calling their name. Show them the treat and then give it to them when you have their attention.

2. Pull out another treat and slowly move it toward their face and then up above their heads, just out of their reach. Say "Sit" as you get the treat into position. If you do this too quickly, they will jump for it.

3. They will need to tilt their heads further and further back to keep the treat in view. This action will automatically require them to sit down. Repeat the word "Sit."

4. The moment that fluffy butt hits the floor, click and treat!

5. Repeat this method a few times until you can stand up straight and get them sitting without having to move your hand.

Bow

This is a simple, fun, cute trick that is relatively easy to train. I like to start off training these playful, easy behaviors first as it gets your puppy comfortable obeying your commands, and they end up with a deeper understanding of training in general. Which greatly helps when it comes to the more difficult things.

1. Get them to focus on you while they are standing up. Click and treat.

2. Touch your treat to their nose and then move it down between their legs, sliding it toward their belly. Say the word "Bow."

3. As soon as they start bowing to get the treat, click, treat, and get them moving. You don't want them to sit or lay down, as it defeats the purpose of training.

4. Keep repeating these steps until you are confident enough to remove the luring aspect. Once you can place the treat directly on the floor and use the cue "Bow," you are all set!

5. If you find that they automatically sit down when you try to refocus them, take two steps backward so that they have to stand up and walk toward you. Then try again.

Down

This is an adorable behavior, and it is the start of teaching your pup to roll over and play dead. Yet, it actually plays a much more important role than being cute. It works well to calm down an anxious or excited dog, and it is a prerequisite for teaching them to "Go to bed" when they misbehave.

Teaching your pup this behavior can become a bit confusing if you have also taught them to bow. I suggest that you master your bow training first, as it can give you a head start in training down if used correctly.

1. Get them into a focused sitting position. Click and treat.

2. Take out a treat and touch it to their nose, move it down to the floor in a straight line until they're standing, bending down. Say the word "Down"

3. Slide the treat across the floor away from them so that they have to lie down to take it. Repeating the word "Down." If you move too quickly, they will likely stand up and try to walk to the treat. You need to master your speed to get it just right.

4. The moment that fluffy tummy hits the deck, click, and treat!

5. Get them back up into a sitting position and repeat the steps above until all you need to do is hold the treat to the floor.

Stay

This is a goodie and so very helpful. Asking your pup to "stay" is not just useful when you want to run into a not-dog-friendly shop during your walk. It can be used for day-to-day activities to stop negative behaviors. I use it during every mealtime.

The moment 4 p.m. hits, my dogs can be found standing by their food bin, waiting in anticipation. This excitement can sometimes get the better of them, and every now and then they may try to jump the line and stick their heads in the bowl before the food is on the floor. By telling them to sit and stay, I can calmly prepare their food without any trouble.

1. Get them into a focused sitting position. Click and treat.

2. Lift your hand up and place your palm out toward their face. Say "Stay" while slowly backing away from them.

3. Take two steps and wait five to ten seconds. Click and treat!

4. Repeat this step, but start taking more and more steps backward before bridging their behavior. See how handy that clicker is becoming? Once bridged, walk back toward them to treat them.

5. If they start to get up and walk toward you, ask them to sit. Once they are sitting, click and reward them for obeying your cue. Start moving back again when you have their focus.

6. You want them to succeed. So, if you find that seven steps back is a bit too much for them to comprehend, stick to six. Once they get the hang of that, you can walk away further.

7. If you would like to incorporate some recall training, you can add the cue "Come!" For this, you will need to repeat the above steps, asking them to stay, walking backward, and using the clicker to bridge the behavior. The only difference is that this time, you are going to say "Come!" the second after you click. They should bound toward you, and you will need to reward them big time. Hugs, a ton of praise, a treat, and even a toy if you would like. This is a big moment, as that little baby genius has just mastered three different behaviors in one go!

Shake or Paw

Shake or Paw is a super easy trick to teach your dog. It's not one of the most important, but it is absolutely adorable! This trick goes against what you are trying to teach them with "leave it." Attempting to train the two at the same time is going to cause mass confusion, and your pup won't be able to learn either. Once you have mastered the one and don't need treats, then you can start the other.

1. Get them into a focused, sitting position. Click and treat.

2. Close a treat in your hand and place it in front of their face. Say "Paw or Shake." They are probably going to get messy now and try to lick and chew their way through your hand. You want them to be frustrated enough to hit you with their paw to get it out.

3. Once they lift their paw to your hand, quickly click and give them a treat from the treat bag. Do not give them your practice treat.

4. Repeat this a few times until they ditch the slobber and only give you their paw.

5. Now you are going to open your hand with no treat it. Tell them "Shake or Paw," and once they give you their paw, click, and treat.

6. Do this a few more times before adding in the shake, and you're done!

Leave It

This is a bit of a difficult one for an impulsive puppy to learn, and if you intend to teach them to shake as well, I suggest you start with that. You need your pup to be a bit more mature and well-versed in other commands to get this right.

Even though it is a little more difficult, it is well worth it, and you can quickly stop your dog from eating some questionable items. This training will become beneficial when you start teaching them to walk nicely!

1. Get them in a focused sitting position. Click and treat.

2. Close your hand around a treat, let your dog sniff it, and ask them to "Leave it." Now you can see where the conflict comes

in when teaching them to shake. You will likely be getting quite a few paw hits before they figure it out.

3. Once they stop trying and choose to wait patiently. Click and give them a treat from the treat bag. Your practice treat shouldn't be used, as it gives them the impression they can still take the item you have asked them to leave, as long as they wait patiently for it.

4. Let's kick the difficulty up a bit by showing them the treat. Open your hand flat with the treat on your palm and say, "Leave it." You are going to need to be quick now, and if they try to take it, close your hand.

5. Once they wait patiently, click and treat!

6. Keep making it more difficult by adding space between the two of you. Put the treat on the floor and take a step back. If they come for the treat, cover it with your foot. When they wait, you guessed it, click and treat.

If your puppy is becoming frustrated, don't push them too hard. Stick to close contact until they master it and then move further away. Switch it up by adding a toy into the mix.

Chapter 8:

Little Legs, Long Walks

It doesn't matter whether you have adopted a 30-pound Olympian or a 4-pound ball of fluff; your pup is likely overflowing with energy. Who can blame them? Everything around them is so exciting and new! This energy can become a little overwhelming, and if not released, your pup will find other, more destructive ways to keep themselves entertained.

Regular walks and runs are a great way to release this energy while keeping your dog fit and healthy. This gives them an opportunity to explore and use all of their senses to take in the enormous amount of information floating in the air. Social interaction and play with other dogs are just an added bonus.

However, it is simply impossible to fit in enough walks in a day to release this energy and keep your dog's mind sharp. You will need to find another way to keep them entertained. This is especially important if you are at work during the day and they are left alone.

Toys, Toys, Toys!

There are so many different types of toys on the market. Thank goodness, because our dogs can be extremely picky when they want to. You may find that your dog is an avid chewer, a ball addict, or one that likes to snuggle up with a fluffy toy. It's best to buy a range of toys to test out, and once you know which ones your dog likes most, invest in a few more of that kind.

Solitary Toys

Solitary play toys are made with just your dog in mind. These keep them entertained during their downtime and give you a second to relax. These include chew toys, squeaky toys, fluffy toys, and puzzles.

They generally come in different sizes to better suit your dog. A small, soft chew toy may be great for a Yorkshire terrier, but it will be torn apart or swallowed whole by a mastiff. You will also need to consider the strength of your toys. A fluffy toy will not be a good idea for a chewer, and some of the more serious chewers might need something a lot stronger than your standard plastic bone. Thankfully, there are brands that make tough toys specifically designed for these kinds of dogs.

Interactive Toys

These can be used for human and dog play or dog and dog play and are great bonding and training tools. Knotted ropes are one of my favorites. They are available pretty much anywhere, or you can make them at home. They come in a variety of sizes, and the fibers and shape of the toy help with teeth cleaning. It was designed for tug of war or toss and catch, but it is fantastic to use as a reward during training as well. If you have a multi-dog household, your dogs can play together.

Balls, balls, balls. You either have a dog that is mind-blowingly obsessed with a tennis ball, or one that gives you that "Are you stupid?" look when you throw one. I have one of each. The best part of playing fetch is the amount of exercise your dog gets in just a few minutes of the game. If you're feeling a bit lazy, you can even buy an automatic ball thrower and teach your dog how to use it. Although, this may not be as exciting for them, as half of the fun comes from you being involved.

Toy wands are not just for cats. Yep, you heard me right; you can actually buy doggie toy wands. The string is much stronger, and so are the toys and feathers on the end. This is not exclusive to small dogs either; buying or making wands that have long ropes can bring a lot of joy to a large pup.

Puzzles and Games

Hide and seek is one of my favorite games to play. I lock him in my bedroom while I hide several treats in and around the house. When I let him loose, he spends hours trying to find them all. This game really gets their minds and noses working and is surprisingly exhausting.

Food puzzles are a fun interactive way to get your dog thinking. There are plenty of different ones on the market, but I like to go old school and use colored plastic cups. I turn them upside down, put a treat under one, and then shuffle them while my dog watches. When he chooses the right cup, he gets the reward. When he selects the wrong cup, the shock on his face is enough to send me into a giggle fit.

Feeder balls make a good solitary play game. These come in different sizes to suit your dog, and they have various holes cut into them. You can fill up the ball with treats or dog food, and your dog has to push the ball around until the right hole is exposed and drops a treat. Most of these toys are adjustable so that you can increase or decrease the activity level for smarter dogs that figure it out too quickly.

Training for Stimulation

Training doesn't just have to be work; it can be fun as well. Dogs thoroughly enjoy cooperative activities, especially ones that lead to your excitement and a treat for them! Working through some of the old tricks they have already mastered is a great way to get them engaged and stimulated. Using these tricks ensures that there is no way your dog can fail, and you are less likely to get frustrated. It's also a fun way to bond, and if the opportunity arises, you can teach them a new trick.

Must-Have Walking Tools

Indoor stimulation is not quite enough. It's time to work on getting those little legs moving and exploring the wild world outside your door. Before you start, there are some important items you will need to have on hand to make the experience as fun and safe as possible.

Leash and Lead

A leash is around 6 ft long and comes in different thicknesses to cater to different-sized dogs. Pick the right one, as one that is too thin is likely to snap if a big dog pulls too hard.

Leads are much, much longer than leashes and are generally used in training. They are perfect for recall training, as they allow your dog to go off quite far from you while you still have control. Leads are also great for secluded outdoor activities such as parks and hiking.

If you are ever in a populated area or dog park, it's best to keep your dog on a leash, especially when they aren't fully trained. You don't know which dogs are reactive or social, and allowing your pup to run up to strange dogs is very irresponsible. Not only does this endanger both dogs, but you could be messing up somebody else's training.

Harness

I much prefer walking my dogs on a harness than a collar. When they pull, the harness applies pressure to the chest rather than the neck, which makes it more comfortable. This allows you greater control over your dog, as they can't slip out of one as easily as a collar. Some come equipped with handles, which are great during emergencies as you can gain full control over your dog immediately.

You can buy front clip or back clip harnesses or ones that come equipped with both. Back clip ones are generally used for dogs that are already pretty good at walking without pulling on the lead. Front clip harnesses work well for training as they allow you to redirect your dog and stop them from pulling.

A harness feels pretty weird at first. I mean, a dog is not exactly used to wearing clothes. So, it may take a little time for them to get used to it.

When you slip it on, adjust the straps so that it fits correctly. You should be able to comfortably fit your fingers under the straps and move them up and down your dog's body. Remember, the more exercise your dog does, the heavier their breathing will become, and their chest will expand. You have to have a bit of space between the harness straps and their chest to accommodate this.

Leave the harness on for an hour or two and regularly reward them when they are calm. Check the sizing again and adjust it if need be. You will need to keep adjusting the harness as they grow, and I suggest buying one that is adjustable enough to at least last their first year. Only once they are comfortable in their gear can you start walking them.

Car Seat Covers

These are an absolute must-have. Whether you and your dog constantly travel, or your car trips are few and between. These will protect your seats from fur and claws while also protecting your pup. The back-side clips on the backseat headrest, and the front piece clips onto the driver and passenger headrest, essentially turning your back seat into a box. This prevents your dog from jumping over into the front seat while you're driving.

If you have a tiny dog, you can buy smaller, box-like covers which confine your dog to a single seat. This will stop them from slipping and falling in the car.

Tools to Avoid

Retractable leads should be avoided at all costs. The constant pressure it places on your dog's neck can be harmful. Despite what the marketing says, they do not actually stop your dog from pulling on the lead while walking. If anything, it worsens it. Your dog will get used to that constant pressure around their necks and think that it's normal. The moment you swap to a normal leash, they will try to replicate the feeling by pulling.

Choke collars were all the rage at one point. Sure, they are a great way to stop your dog from running away, but it's also a great way to cause some serious damage to their spinal cord and windpipe. Other than injury, using choke collars will ruin what should be a fun experience, and I will be surprised if your dog gets excited to go for a walk again.

Can We Go Yet?

Before you head straight out that gate into the big, scary world, you will need to do some practice and preparation. If you are lucky, your dog will take to it immediately, but let's be real here; they are probably going to tug on the leash in a panic when they realize they can't actually get away from you.

The steps below may seem long, boring, and unnecessary. Even if you do find them boring, I promise you; they are definitely necessary. Taking your puppy out on a walk too early and with no training can lead to a traumatizing experience for both of you. You need them to be confident and feel safe with you before they explore new areas.

Baby Steps

Training your puppy to heel is easy enough as long as you have enough time and patience. The goal of this training is to get your dog to walk in a controlled manner at your side. This training will greatly decrease the chances of your dog pulling on their leash when you get to walking.

Step One: Peace and Quiet

Puppies have the attention span of a goldfish, so when it comes to training, you don't want any distractions, loud noises, other pets, or human beings. Find a quiet spot in your house or yard. The quieter it is, the more your puppy will be able to focus on you.

Step Two: Get in Position

Stand with your dog on one side. If you choose for them to be on the left, then hold your click in your right hand and your treats in your left. Ask your dog to sit and focus on you. Click and treat to reward them. Try to keep this focus for at least a minute before you start moving.

Step Three: Bait Them!

Hold a treat in front of their face, but don't let them have it just yet. Walk two steps forward while saying "Heel" and wait for them to follow you. After these steps, click and treat. You want to keep them as close to you as possible, so try to hold the treat right by your knees. Higher or lower is fine, depending on your dog's height.

Step Four: Rinse and Repeat

Keep your sessions short; ten-minute sessions spread throughout the day should be more than enough. You can now spread out your treats a little more. Reward them every five steps, then every ten, and so on until you can cut the treats out completely.

Once you are happy with their progress, you can introduce the leash.

Toddler Steps

You want to teach your pup that pulling on the leash is the fastest way to get them nowhere at all. The moment they pull, and you allow it, the behavior will continue and become harder to fix. Let's go through some simple steps to get your pup walking like an angel.

Step One: Pulling Gets You Nowhere

Clip the lead on and start your heel training. After a few meters, quit the treats and continue to walk as normal in a straight line, giving them the full length of the leash. When they stay by your side, and the leash is loose, click and treat.

If they start to wander off from your path, let them but stand still just before the leash tightens up. They are going to turn around to try to figure out what on earth you have stopped for, but you will need to stay in position.

When they pay attention to you or return, reward them and start walking again. You will need to practice this in short but consistent sessions for the next few days.

If you find that your dog is struggling to understand what they have to do when you stop, go back to your heel training again. You want to set them up to succeed, and if that means repeating the basics, so be it.

Step Two: Hold Your Leash Correctly

Your dog is not a mind reader, and if they are walking in front of you, they don't know that you intend to turn until they feel the tug at their neck to bring them back.

Save yourself the hassle and your dog the confusion by using your leash correctly. If your dog is on your right-hand side, you want your leash in your left hand. Your right hand will steer your pup in the direction that you want them to go in. When you want to turn, you will move your hand down the leash until you reach your knees. Applying some gentle pressure will bring their focus back to you and direct their bodies in the direction you would like to go.

Step Three: Keep Their Focus

Dogs are creatures of habit, and if you only train in a straight line, they will continue to walk that straight line. They begin to anticipate your movements and aren't actually focusing on you at all. This can become problematic if they catch sight of something more interesting or if you want to quickly change your routes.

The best way to train them to focus is by making your movements unpredictable.

Start your training as normal, walk forward until you can see they have gotten into their old routine, and then suddenly turn them and walk back the way you came. When you turn, you will need to steer them using the method in step two. I prefer to use the vocal cue "U-turn!" as well to make sure that I have their full attention.

Whenever you feel you are losing their focus, try this trick and make sure to give them a reward for obeying.

SQUIRREL!

One of the things we don't prepare for is the sudden, extremely exciting moment that your dog catches sight of prey. If you have a dog with a high prey drive, prepare to run. If you aren't a great runner, make sure you are wearing knee and elbow pads; you are going for a ride. Even if you have adopted a soft nature pooch, the intrigue will be enough to stop them in their tracks, and it can be really difficult to get them out of the trance.

This is where recall training is beneficial.

Step One: Teaching Manners

To start recall training, you need to teach your pup that they can't barge through and take whatever they want. This is difficult and requires a lot of restraint from them. This training should be started early in life, but don't be surprised if very young puppies aren't capable of containing their excitement.

What you are going to do is repeat your walking training as usual, but this time you are going to add in multiple exciting objects such as toys, food, and treats. These should be far enough away from you that your pup can't snatch them when they walk past but close enough that they can see them.

As you walk, your pup will veer off course and head toward the closest toy. Stand dead still. They will realize they can't get further and turn and look at you for guidance. Call them back, click, and then reward them with the object they were going for.

This basic training teaches them that they can get what they want as long as they have enough manners to ask you first.

Step Two: What's My Name Again?

Time for actual recall training. You need your dog to feel that coming back to you is more rewarding than what they are trying to run after.

For this, you will need to pull out your long lead and allow them some extra freedom.

Wait for them to move far off, and then, in a super excited, crazy voice, call them back to you. You should be patting your legs and shouting their name, and doing a little dance. Whatever it takes to get them excited enough to come back.

When they do, click and reward. This time, your rewards will not be one boring treat. Give them something special! I like to use a toy as a reward and have a short game of tug and war. Give them treats and toys if you need to.

Step Three: Rinse and Repeat

Keep this up for a few sessions and then increase the difficulty by putting them into a more distracting environment. Your lead is still on, which means that if they do decide to try to bolt, you still have control and can bring them back if needed. You may find that in these situations, your dog returns to you but struggles to maintain focus. If this happens, grab the lead and start to walk them in the opposite direction until you get their full attention.

Recall training is not a once-off. You will need to keep this up throughout their life. Do it during your walks and at home, even if you don't need to.

Which Way Should We Go?

Alright, you are now confident in your training and your dog's abilities. It's time to venture out. I suggest that you pick out a nice, quiet route. One that can accommodate a quick, short walk but can be lengthened as your training advances. Walk the route alone at first and take note of anything that might be frightening or intriguing to your dog. For example, do you walk past any parks, is the road very busy, or are there any dogs that bark at you from their yard? If you answer yes to any of these, figure out how you will help your puppy to remain calm when they walk past these obstacles. If you can't, it's best to pick out another route for now.

This might sound a little paranoid, but I find that it helps me to feel confident on my walks, and that's what you need to be to keep your puppy feeling confident as well!

Rinse and Repeat

Keeping up a routine is the next step and one of the most important ones. Not only is this routine sure to keep you and your pup healthy, but it will also keep them comfortable with the activity. Your puppy is in a vital learning stage, and the associations they make at this point will continue with them through life. Allowing too much time between walks allows the growth of fear, and a puppy that felt comfortable walking two weeks ago might feel different about it today!

Chapter 9:

Powering Through the Toddler

Stage

Okay, I knew it would be a bumpy road to success, but this road is full of potholes! I obeyed the rules and hid my shoes to remove the chewing temptation, but nobody told me I would have to hide my toilet paper, sofa, and water bottle too. Yet as I find myself on the verge of screaming and evicting this infuriating pup of mine, he shoots me the most adorable, apologetic look. How could I not forgive him?

There is a very popular saying in puppy training, and that is, "Just relax; they will grow out of it." I am here to assure you that they won't.

Your pup is currently in their boundary-pushing toddler months, and what they are doing is completely natural. If they were still with their mom, she would warn their behavior off with a growl or even a nip! Inviting them into your family means that you need to take control, become that mother figure, and help them to figure out what is wrong and right.

Don't worry; there are tons of positive ways to create boundaries without you having to bare your teeth and nip them…

Stop That!

Puppies are adorable, and even when they do something wrong, we can't help but forgive them when they flash us those big puppy dog eyes. The thing is… puppies grow up, and the behaviors you thought were cute are suddenly extremely problematic. Each time you reward their negative behaviors and choose not to fix them, you are reinforcing the idea that what they are doing is right.

Imagine the turmoil they will go through later in life when they find out that what they have been doing for all these years is actually wrong!

My Mouth Hurts

Chewing is a super common behavioral issue in puppies, and generally, it's due to teething. This can be incredibly painful, and chewing on things around the house can relieve the pain. While plenty of puppies do actually grow out of this behavior once the pain subsides, others continue to do it out of habit and because they simply don't know better.

By providing them with an alternative solution to the problem, you can save your Louis Vuittons and reduce the chance of the behavior reoccurring in the future.

Chew toys are the obvious solution here, but not all of them will work in this situation. Shoes are usually the first casualty in your dog's murder spree. This is because they are soft and pliable, which makes them gentle enough to chew without causing pain but hard enough to relieve the pressure. Purchase chew toys of a similar texture and softness. If they need a little more motivation to move over to their new toys, spread some peanut butter over them to entice them!

There are other ways to help your pup through this painful stage. Giving them ice cubes can soothe their gums, and it makes for some fun play time. Rubbing teething gel onto their gums will help stop the pain for a moment. Do this regularly if you find that they are really struggling.

Finally, kibble can be a bit harsh on those swollen gums. Consider switching them to canned or wet food for a while.

Your Hands Are Tasty

Mouthing is the ultimate puppy behavior. It seems so cute at first until their sharp little puppy teeth dig into your skin. I swear those little needles are more painful than their adult teeth! Mouthing usually occurs when your pooch is going through their teething stage. However, it also marks a critical moment in their social development. Puppies will mouth or nip to process information, test boundaries, and play.

You will need to teach them your boundaries and provide them with an outlet to release this energy. Chew toys are a great start, but the toys aren't as entertaining as you. Encouraging the behavior by giggling or turning it into a game is only going to worsen it! Ignoring their behavior and removing your hand or leaving the room entirely when they try to chew on you will show them that they will not get any reaction out of you when they do it.

Another way to discourage this behavior is by reacting dramatically when they mouth you. Allow them to chew on your hand without reaction for a few seconds and then shout OW! And quickly remove your hand. This will show your dog that what they have done has hurt you.

Pay Attention to Me!

Dogs will often seek attention by whining, nudging or barking at you. This can become very frustrating, especially when you are trying your best to concentrate on something important. Before you can remedy this behavior, you need to figure out why your dog is exhibiting it in the first place. There are basically four reasons why your dog behaves negatively, and attention-seeking can be caused by one of these. A lack of mental stimulation, a lack of socialization, a lack of physical stimulation, and a lack of attention in general from their owners.

Each of these problems are easily solvable, and I won't waste your time going over the obvious solutions. Instead, let's look at what happens when you reinforce their attention-seeking.

We often reinforce this behavior without knowing it. If your dog is whining, and you turn, pat their heads, then turn around and continue to ignore them, you have rewarded it. Your dog has not gotten what they needed out of that interaction with you, and you have not listened to what they were trying to tell you. They will continue to display this behavior and take pleasure in the small amounts of attention they do get from you.

This can become more difficult to fix, but it's best to start with the basics. By keeping your dog stimulated and emotionally satisfied, the attention-seeking will likely stop or at least slow. The remaining behaviors are just a consequence of habit, and it's best to ignore your dog completely when they start to beg.

This is called extinction training. Extinction training requires you to do absolutely nothing whatsoever. You just need to ignore the unwanted behavior that your dog is displaying. By ignoring it and not rewarding it, your dog will realize that it is useless to continue using this method to get your attention.

Extinction training requires a lot of self-control on your part, and if you give in, you will need to start the process all over again. I always recommend using extinction training with positive reinforcement. Reward your dog when they stop whining and sit calmly. This reinforces your approval of their calm, quiet behavior, and they are more likely to act this way in the future.

Hello, Can You Hear Me?

Yap, yap, yap! Just be quiet already!! We have all been here, and we have all screamed those exact words. That yapping, especially puppy yapping, for some reason. It feels like somebody is drilling into your brain. Puppies, much like kids, don't really have filters yet, and they are using every new bark they have in their vocabulary.

There are a few reasons why your pup may bark excessively; the first is due to attention seeking, which we have already discussed. The second is due to boredom. If your pup is bored, they are going to find a way to entertain themselves, and if that entertainment comes from you pulling your hair out, then so be it. This is easy enough to solve. Give them things to play with! When they become distracted, direct them back to their toy box and get them playing again.

Finally, this barking could be a fear response. Follow them when they bark and try to pinpoint what they are actually barking at. You may find that it's something as silly as an owl statue in your backyard. By removing the fear or showing your dog that they don't need to be scared, you can cure your barking madness.

This Is MY Food!

Food guarding is a common behavioral problem in dogs and puppies. This is just one type of resource guarding, and some dogs may go as far as to protect their beds, toys, and even humans! Rescued dogs will likely have a sense of abandonment and will try to keep what little they have protected. It can take a while for these lost souls to feel truly comfortable and relaxed in a new home.

Dogs that live in a multi-pet household are probably dealing with a lot of competition and are more likely to protect their special items. It's understandable for them to feel this way. We react the same way when our roommates take something that isn't theirs! Yet, when this happens, we, for some reason, still take away the toy they are guarding as a punishment. This is only making it worse as it creates an even stronger need for them to protect their things!

If you are dealing with this situation in a multi-pet household, then you will need to buy more of everything. Having enough toys, beds, and games to go around is the best option. If you have three dogs, and they compete for one toy. Buy two more of those. Don't let there be a need for the competition in the first place.

When it comes to food guarding, you may find that one dog is actually hogging the other's food, and your pup that ends up food guarding is doing so because they are hungry. Establish mealtimes and watch your dogs from start to finish, ensuring that everyone is able to get enough. If you need to, separate your dogs for the first few weeks so that they can become more comfortable.

Chapter 10:

Building Confidence and

Conquering Fear

Fears are generally only noticeable in dogs when they reach their adult years. This is mainly because their reactions to these fears are more prominent and destructive. In fact, the majority of these fears manifest when your dog is just a puppy. Puppies go through two major fear stages during their development.

The first stage occurs between two and three weeks of age, and the second between eight and eleven weeks. These periods are part of vital survival techniques, and the fears they developed in the wild would often become the difference between life and death. If they never learn to have a fear of fire, they would constantly be burned. A domestic situation is a little different, and they can end up being afraid of things they don't need to actually worry about. This is where we need to step in and ensure that they pass through these stages unharmed.

Understanding Fear

Before you can begin helping your dog to heal and overcome these fears, you need to figure out why they have developed in the first place. The cause is usually easy to identify when you really think about it.

Why is My Dog Scared?

Bad experiences are the top cause of fear. If your dog has been attacked or hurt by a person or dog, it's understandable that they will develop a fear and avoid social encounters. During their fear stages, something as simple as a smack from a ticked-off cat can trigger a lifelong fear response.

Isolation

Puppies that have been too isolated have never had the chance to actually experience positive and negative situations. They have never been able to learn and adapt their responses to these stimuli. Their emotional, mental, and social development has been stunted, and they simply can't cope with new experiences.

Isolation fears have become increasingly common in what we now jokingly call Covid-19 puppies. These puppies were adopted either just before or during the Covid-19 lockdowns, and their owners were unable to walk or socialize them correctly.

Incorrect Training

We all make mistakes; it's only human, and occasionally, our mistakes can instill fear in our pups. Using positive punishment and negative reinforcement is guaranteed to cause your dog to develop some sort of fear. It may not be noticeable at first, but the cracks will begin to show later in life.

Incorrect positive reinforcement can be just as bad. If you are rewarding your dog at the wrong time, you could be creating a positive association with the fear they are experiencing. Essentially, validating their negative feelings and allowing them to grow.

Common Fears

There are loads of different fears that your dog may develop through life, but it would be impossible to actually work through each one. While each dog has their personal experiences and trauma, their genetic makeup makes them more prone to the following common fears.

What Was That Bang?

There aren't many dogs that aren't petrified of loud noises or bangs. It's no surprise, their hearing is twice as good as ours! Even a car backfiring can send them into a barking frenzy. Some dogs begin to understand what these noises are and that they won't harm them. Others will live their entire lives with the firm belief that thunder has a personal vendetta against them.

Stranger Danger

This is not always a bad thing; you don't really want your dog to greet robbers with a cup of cocoa. However, it can become problematic when your pup fears everyone. There is no way for them to escape human and dog contact forever, and the constant stress can have some serious health implications.

Where Are We??

Again, a fear of strange new places is not unusual. All dogs should feel a sense of wonder and intrigue with a healthy dose of caution. As with all fears, there are levels, and an extreme fear can cause your dog to flee the scene or become aggressive if you hold them back. This type of fear usually occurs in dogs that have been isolated, and they are just so overwhelmed by the amount of new information.

Don't Leave Me Alone!

Separation anxiety is very common in rescue dogs that have been abandoned or given away to a new family. The trauma of being dumped like this causes them to have an unhealthy attachment to you, as they fear you may do the same. Although, boredom at home or negative experiences that you don't know happen when you are gone can also trigger separation anxiety as your dog looks to you as their protector.

Dogs with separation anxiety will often become destructive and destroy furniture. In extreme cases, they will become so desperate to get to you that they actually break through windows or scratch through doors.

What Happens If I Leave It?

Well, nothing good. A state of fear releases adrenaline, and your dog can only react in one of two ways when they reach their threshold. Fight or flight. The flight response is one of the scariest for us, as dogs can run at lightning speeds and scale walls like Spider-Man when they need to! At this point, recall training doesn't work, and it can be difficult to get them back.

Fight, on the other hand, can be just as dangerous. If you are holding your dog in a scary situation, they may turn and bite you to break free. Being stuck in a position with a strange person or dog, with no chance to flee, can cause your dog to attack. In their minds, It's their life or the strangers and in those situations, they will choose theirs.

Just A Big Ball of Anxiety and Reactivity

One fear leads to another, and another and another until your dog is a walking, barking ball of anxiety. A fear of strange people can suddenly lead to a fear of the dogs they are walking. This can lead to a fear of being in the park in the first place, which can lead to a fear of getting into the car. It's one big domino chain!

If your dog has hit this point, it is going to take a ton of work to get them back to the confident state they need to be in to be happy.

Shaping a Confident Puppy

Confidence is key! Your puppy will never be able to conquer their fears unless they are confident enough in themselves and their abilities to handle any situation. They require a lot of support and look to you as their protector. This means it's your job to guide them through this turmoil and show them that there is light on the other side of the tunnel.

Flooding

Flooding is a term used to describe overloading a dog with information or stimuli. It was once and still is used as a treatment for humans and dogs alike. The goal of flooding is to constantly expose them to a fearful stimulus until they are unable to be physically aroused by it anymore. Essentially getting used to the stimulus and losing their fear. An example would be locking your dog in a room and playing recordings of thunder until they stop reacting. The problem is that while the dog does stop reacting, it's because they are physically and mentally exhausted and have simply given up and accepted their fate.

While humans can understand and agree to such treatments, dogs are left in the dark with no idea what they did to you to deserve such a harsh punishment. Imagine trapping an unwilling person with crippling arachnophobia in a room full of spiders? They may stop screaming, but they will need a straitjacket and a trip to the hospital afterward. This is not a healthy way to treat fear!

In positive reinforcement training, we try our best to avoid flooding our dogs and instead use counter-conditioning or desensitization. This way, we can help them overcome their fears in a slow, comfortable way to build their confidence rather than destroy their spirit.

Love, Love, Love

There often seems to be confusion when you tell a person to love their dog during stressful periods. Love does not mean pampering them or soothing them when they are scared. Love means listening to them, protecting them and guiding them through the fear, and finding an appropriate solution.

An easy example would be a dog that is terrified during a thunderstorm. Sitting on the floor with them, rubbing their heads, and saying, "I'm sorry, baby, I'm sorry..." will only make things worse. You are focusing their attention on the stimulus and confirming their feelings of fear. They begin to react in an even more fearful way, which causes you to soothe them even more.

A better solution would be to take charge of the situation! You have listened to what they have told you; they are scared. Protect them by moving them to a quieter room and closing the windows and doors. Guide them through it by distracting them with a fun game or toy, and reward them when you see they are enjoying themselves and not as focused on the storm outside.

You have not confirmed their fear; you have lessened the stimulus and found a way to show them that life goes on and can be enjoyed, even when the wind is howling outside.

Counterconditioning and Desensitization

Counter-conditioning and desensitization go hand in hand. Desensitization involves slowly exposing your dog to a fearful stimulus, while counter-conditioning involves changing your dog's response to that stimulus.

Let's continue with our thunder example and work through how you could desensitize your dog to this sound. First, you are going to need some recordings of thunder. YouTube is here for you and will surely provide some fantastic ones. Then, grab some of the most delicious treats that you can find and pick up some of your dog's favorite toys as well.

1. Take your dog into a calm room with no distractions. Get their attention by giving them a treat. It's best to uplift their moods, so play a little game before you start.

2. Turn on the recording of the thunder at a very low volume. Your dog's ears are going to immediately perk up, and they will display their usual fearful behavior.

3. You are going to change your dog's reaction to the noise by creating a positive association with it. Give them tons of treats and play some games until they are relaxed.

4. Repeat this step with the recordings at this volume for a few days. If you play the recording and your dog immediately looks at you with a happy face, expecting a reward, you can advance to the next level.

5. Turn the volume up a little more, and monitor your dogs' response. Repeat the above steps and reward them continuously throughout the process.

6. Repeat these steps, increasing the volume a tiny bit each time.

7. If you notice that you are unable to get your dog's attention and the fear is just too much, turn the volume down again and work at a threshold that they are comfortable with. This is not a quick process, and if you try to rush it, you can make their fear worse.

This kind of training can solve just about any fear your dog has. You only need to switch it up a little. If your dog is fearful of humans, introduce a stranger to them the same way you introduced the thunder. Keep them far away while you reward your dog. Ask the person to approach one step at a time while you continue to reward your pooch. After a few sessions, they may have just found their new human best friend!

You can also incorporate your clicker into this situation. The clicker means reward, so every time your dog glances at the stranger, click immediately and give them a treat. Use this method carefully, as you need to be quick! If you click too late, you may be rewarding the fearful response to that person.

Conclusion

Alright, let's swing right back into the happy stuff. Your book journey is over for now, but your puppy adventure has just begun. You are about to enter the most rewarding and downright adorable years of your life. I can't imagine anything more exciting!

Hopefully, I have been able to walk you through everything you need to know about finding your soul mate, how to feed them, and care for them when they are feeling ill. The foundations to become the perfect pet parent. The most important thing is that you have learned how to shape an emotionally stable, healthy, and obedient puppy that will be able to share years and years of joy with you. Everything you do together, whether it's car rides, training, adventures, or simple snuggles, should be strengthening your relationship, not breaking it down. If you find that you have made a mistake, which you are bound to! Don't let it get you down. Work through the steps to build your puppy's confidence back up and try again.

The responsibility of owning a pup can be quite overwhelming at first, and you should never feel ashamed to seek help if you need it. If you work long hours or if you are just worried about them being alone, save yourself the guilt and look into puppy daycare or a pet nanny. If grandma gets just as lonely, take advantage of the free labor and find out if she would be interested in caring for your baby while you're out! There are loads of solutions, and it is worth exploring each one before you become frazzled.

When you do feel like you have hit a wall, especially in training, take a deep breath, have a cup of tea, and come back for another read. There may be something you missed, and if I haven't covered it, there are tons of resources out there that can help you find the solution to your problem. If you find that you just need a shoulder to cry on, think about joining a puppy training class or one of the many social media puppy owner groups. These are fantastic safe spaces where you can share your struggles without judgment and learn new tips and tricks from others that have gone through the same thing.

The first few weeks are the hardest, but once you get into the rhythm of things, you won't even be able to remember the last time you felt unhappy. Cherish these puppy months, their adorable baby howls, their floppy ears, and those sharp little baby teeth. Embrace their mistakes, their successes, and all the unique behaviors that make your special bundle of joy.

If your puppy has enjoyed this book, please help to leave a pawsome review on Amazon!

Author Bio

I can't remember a time in my life when I was not completely obsessed with dogs! Especially the ones that nobody else wants. Growing up, I had to constantly resist the urge to bring home every stray puppy I saw, and each time, my heart broke a little more. When the opportunity finally arose for me to provide one of these lost souls with the perfect home, I drove straight to the shelter.

However, nobody ever told me that puppies were so difficult to look after. Especially the ones that had only ever experienced heartbreak. My house was a mess; my life was turned upside down. I barely slept, and I cried on and off for two weeks! I had brought this broken little one into my life with the promise of fixing, protecting, and loving them, only to realize that I had no idea how.

I dried my tears and set out to learn the best way to train and heal my new soulmate. Inspired by my favorite behaviorists and dog trainers, I decided to follow in their footsteps and help as many people and pups as possible.

For the last 30 years, I have dedicated my time to studying different training techniques—the good, the bad, and the ugly—and I came to learn exactly which ones produced the results I wanted. The end goal is never just a trained dog. The goal is a well-adjusted, healthy, and happy dog.

I soon learned that training them was easy, but losing them is hard. When my Gizmo slipped into his senior years, my world was turned upside down. I was so focused on the present that I hadn't put any thought into the future. In those last years, our roles were reversed. He became the trainer, and I, the trainee. The lessons I learned from him have stayed with me forever and prepared me for the inevitable love and loss I would experience again and again.

My books are compiled of tried and true techniques, life lessons, and healthy coping mechanisms that have personally helped me to work with and love my dogs. I am confident that I can provide them the best life from puppy to senior that they deserve, and by the time you finish reading this, you will be too.

—Hope Chambers

References

Agadoni, L. (2022, March 18). *How to help a scared dog overcome their fears.* Care. https://www.care.com/c/how-to-help-your-scared-dog-overcome-his-fear/

AKC Staff. (2019a, July 15). *Your Complete Guide to First-Year Puppy Vaccinations.* American Kennel Club. https://www.akc.org/expert-advice/health/puppy-shots-complete-guide/

AKC Staff. (2019b, September 26). *AKC Groups: Sporting, Hound, Working, Terrier, Toy, Non-Sporting, Herding.* American Kennel Club. https://www.akc.org/expert-advice/lifestyle/7-akc-dog-breed-groups-explained/

AKC Staff. (2020, March 3). *Proper Puppy Nutrition Nourishes Rapid Growth & Development.* American Kennel Club. https://www.akc.org/expert-advice/health/proper-puppy-nutrition-nourishes-rapid-growth/

AKC Staff. (2021, September 28). *How to Stop Puppy Biting.* American Kennel Club. https://www.akc.org/expert-advice/training/stop-puppy-biting/

AKC Staff. (2022a, January 1). *Puppy Schedule: Daily Routine for New Puppies.* American Kennel Club. https://www.akc.org/expert-advice/training/setting-schedules-and-developing-a-routine-for-your-new-puppy/#:~:text=Keep%20to%20a%20regular%20routine

AKC Staff. (2022b, December 13). *A Survival Guide for Dog Diarrhea.* American Kennel Club. https://www.akc.org/expert-advice/health/doggie-diarrhea/#:~:text=Withholding%20food%20for%2012%20to

Alvarez, L. (2022, November 16). *How Much Should You Feed Your Puppy? A Complete Puppy Feeding Chart.* The Honest Kitchen. https://www.thehonestkitchen.com/blogs/pet-wellness/puppy-feeding-chart

Annerike. (2021, March 7). *Raising and caring for puppies: 20 clever tips.* Prins Petfoods. https://www.prinspetfoods.com/advice-info/raising-and-caring-for-puppies

Ansorge, R. (2021, May 8). *Nutritional Needs of Puppies.* Fetch. https://pets.webmd.com/dogs/feeding-puppy

Aquanta. (n.d.). *A General Guide to Puppy Safety.* Dog Health. https://www.doghealth.com/care/safety/2329-a-general-guide-to-puppy-safety

Ardente, A. (2023, January 17). *How To Choose the Right Food for Your Puppy.* PetMD. https://www.petmd.com/dog/nutrition/best-puppy-food

Arford, K. (2020, October 20). *10 Science-Based Benefits of Having a Dog.* American Kennel Club. https://www.akc.org/expert-advice/lifestyle/10-science-based-benefits-dog/

Arford, K. (2021a, September 1). *Dog First-Aid Kit Essentials: What To Include For Injuries And Emergencies.* American Kennel Club. https://www.akc.org/expert-advice/health/dog-first-aid-kit-essentials/

Arford, K. (2021b, September 2). *The Best and Worst Toys for A Teething Puppy.* American Kennel Club. https://www.akc.org/expert-advice/health/best-puppy-toys/

Arnold, B. (2020, September 14). *How to Train Your Kids (To Be Exceptional Dog Owners)*. The Dogington Post. https://www.dogingtonpost.com/train-your-kids-dogs/

Asher, M. (2020, February 20). *Dog Training Methods And 5 Essential Dog Obedience Commands*. Pets Best. https://www.petsbest.com/blog/dog-training-basic-commands/

Ashley, S. A. (2020, April 6). *Dog Body Language: 45 Ways Your Dog Is Secretly Communicating with You*. PureWow. https://www.purewow.com/family/dog-body-language

ASPCA. (n.d.). *Mouthing, Nipping and Biting in Puppies*. ASPCA. https://www.aspca.org/pet-care/dog-care/common-dog-behavior-issues/mouthing-nipping-and-biting-puppies#:~:text=Either%20ignore%20him%20for%2010

ASPCA. (2014, September 25). *House Training Your Dog or Puppy*. ASPCA. https://www.aspca.org/news/house-training-your-dog-or-puppy

ASPCA. (2015a). *Food Guarding*. ASPCA. https://www.aspca.org/pet-care/dog-care/common-dog-behavior-issues/food-guarding

ASPCA. (2015b). *People Foods to Avoid Feeding Your Pets*. ASPCA. https://www.aspca.org/pet-care/animal-poison-control/people-foods-avoid-feeding-your-pets

ASPCA. (2022). *Pet Statistics*. ASPCA. https://www.aspca.org/helping-people-pets/shelter-intake-and-surrender/pet-statistics

Australia, B. P. (n.d.). *Tired of yapping? How to stop nuisance dog barking*. Buddy Pet Australia. https://buddypet.co/blogs/learn/tired-of-yapping-how-to-stop-nuisance-dog-barking

Australian Veterinary Association. (2019, October 9). *What to do if your pet vomits or has diarrhoea*. Vet Voice.

https://www.vetvoice.com.au/articles/what-to-do-if-your-pet-vomits-or-has-diarrhoea/

BatterSea. (2016, October 4). *Toxic food for dogs.* Batter Sea. https://www.battersea.org.uk/pet-advice/dog-care-advice/toxic-food-dogs

Battersea. (2020a, February 21). *How to teach your dog not to jump up.* Battersea. https://www.battersea.org.uk/pet-advice/dog-advice/how-teach-your-dog-not-jump

Battersea. (2020b, October 14). *How to stop my puppy mouthing.* Battersea. https://www.battersea.org.uk/pet-advice/dog-advice/how-stop-my-puppy-mouthing

Battersea. (2021, March 15). *How to Stop Your Dog Barking.* Battersea. https://www.battersea.org.uk/pet-advice/dog-advice/how-stop-your-dog-barking#:~:text=Stay%20silent%20and%20don

Bauhaus, J. M. (2021, August 19). *How to Clean Dog Ears.* Hill's Pet Nutrition. https://www.hillspet.com/dog-care/routine-care/how-to-clean-dog-ears#:~:text=Use%20a%20cotton%20ball%20or

Becker, M. (2022, September 21). *Dog Training 101: Essential Tools You'll Need.* Vetstreet. https://www.vetstreet.com/our-pet-experts/dog-training-101-essential-tools-youll-need

Bell, J. S. (2017, September 25). *Ten Most Common Hereditary Diseases in Dogs.* World Small Animal Veterinary Association Congress Proceedings, 2017. World Small Animal Veterinary Association Congress Proceedings. https://www.vin.com/doc/?id=8506247

Bergel, H. (2021, February 12). *How to Teach a Puppy to Walk on Leash.* Daily Paws. https://www.dailypaws.com/dogs-puppies/dog-training/basic/how-to-teach-a-puppy-to-walk-on-leash

Best Behaviour Dog Training. (2022, April 29). *Dogs are a big commitment - do you have time?* Best Behaviour Dog Training. https://www.bestbehaviourdogtraining.co.uk/blog-post/Time-for-a-dog/

Beverly Hills Vet. (2018, October 30). *Scaredy-Dog: Common Dog Fears.* Beverly Hills Veterinary Associates. https://www.beverlyhillsvets.com/blog/scaredy-dog-common-dog-fears/

Blue Valley Animal Hospital. (2022, June 9). *The Importance of Dog Vaccines.* Blue Valley Animal Hospital. https://www.bluevalleyanimalhospital.net/blog/the-importance-of-dog-vaccines/

Blyth, T. (n.d.). *What is the socialisation Period?* KC College. https://www.tarynblyth.co.za/what-is-the-socialisation-period

Boecker, A. (2019, February 4). *Puppy School: Yes or No? (How useful is it really?).* Hundeo: Dog Training. https://www.hundeo.com/en/training/puppy-training/puppy-school/

Brown, A. (2022, November 11). *What dog owners need to know about the four training quadrants.* Koru K9 Dog Training. https://www.koruk9.com/tips-and-tricks/what-dog-owners-need-to-know-about-the-four-training-quadrants/#:~:text=The%20four%20quadrants%20are%20Positive

Burke, A. (2018, July 3). *Common Fears and Phobias in Dogs and How to Help Treat Them.* American Kennel Club. https://www.akc.org/expert-advice/training/common-fears-and-phobias-in-dogs/

Burke, A. (2021, June 21). *Dog Coughing: Causes and Treatment Options.* American Kennel Club. https://www.akc.org/expert-advice/health/dog-coughing-causes-treatment/

Callahan, K. (2022, March 22). *No Need for Force | How to Get Dog to Stop Pulling on Leash.* Whole Dog Journal. https://www.whole-dog-journal.com/training/how-to-stop-your-dog-from-pulling-on-the-leash/

Carr, E. C. J., Wallace, J. E., Pater, R., & Gross, D. P. (2019). Evaluating the Relationship between Well-Being and Living with a Dog for People with Chronic Low Back Pain: A Feasibility Study. *International Journal of Environmental Research and Public Health,* 16(8), 1472. https://doi.org/10.3390/ijerph16081472

Cesar's Way. (2016, March 22). *Ultimate Raising A Puppy Guide.* Cesar's Way. https://www.cesarsway.com/puppy-101-the-ultimate-guide-to-raising-a-puppy/

Chewy Editorial. (2018, July 2). *5 Common Congenital Dog Diseases.* BeChewy. https://be.chewy.com/5-common-genetic-diseases-of-dogs/

Chewy Editorial. (2023, March 22). *Puppy Feeding Guide: How Much to Feed a Puppy & More.* BeChewy. https://be.chewy.com/puppy-feeding-guide/

Clancy, M. (2020, March 31). *13 Essential Items To Have In Your Dog's First-Aid Kit.* Dogtime. https://dogtime.com/dog-health/general/21573-things-in-dog-first-aid-kit

Clark, M. (2019, January 10). *7 Most Popular Dog Training Methods.* Dogtime. https://dogtime.com/reference/dog-training/50743-7-popular-dog-training-methods

Clason, D. (2022, November 15). *Steps you can take to stop the bad behavior of leash pulling*. PawTracks. https://www.pawtracks.com/dogs/leash-pulling-training/

Clur, K.-B. (2022, June 8). *10 Best Vitamins and Supplements for Puppies in 2023*. Pet Keen. https://petkeen.com/best-vitamins-supplements-for-puppies/

Companion Animal Psychology. (2021, May 26). *Top Tips on Puppy Raising from the Experts (Guide)*. Companion Animal Psychology. https://www.companionanimalpsychology.com/2021/05/top-tips-on-puppy-raising-from-experts.html

Comstock, J. (2022, June 23). *How to Socialize a Puppy & Why It's So Important*. Daily Paws. https://www.dailypaws.com/dogs-puppies/dog-training/basic/how-to-socialize-a-puppy

Crittenden, C. (2021, October 25). *5 Basic Commands Every Dog Should Know (And How to Teach Them)*. Petful. https://www.petful.com/behaviors/basic-commands-your-dog-should-know/

The Dog Blog. (2023, March 13). *Monitoring a Healthy Weight for Your Puppy*. Bil-Jac. https://www.bil-jac.com/the-dog-blog/posts/monitoring-a-healthy-weight-for-your-puppy/

Dog Sense. (2020, March 30). *21 (Super Easy) Ways To Mentally Stimulate Your Dog*. Dog Sense. https://dogsense.co.nz/mental-stimulation-for-dogs/

Dog Trust. (n.d.-a). *How to stop your dog pulling on the lead*. Dog Trust. https://www.dogstrust.org.uk/dog-advice/training/outdoors/walking-nicely-training

Dog Trust. (n.d.-b). *How to stop your dog resource guarding food and toys*. Dog Trust. https://www.dogstrust.org.uk/dog-advice/training/unwanted-behaviours/resource-guarding-food-and-toys

Dog Zen. (2016, December 8). *Choosing the best puppy from a litter.* Dog Zen. https://dogzen.com/choosing-a-puppy/

Doggy Treat Box Blog. (2021, September 30). *Puppy essentials, What equipment you need for your new puppy.* Doggy Treat Box. https://doggytreatbox.com/puppy-essentials-what-equipment-you-need-for-your-new-puppy/

Donovan, L. (2019a, July 30). *Leash Train Your Puppy In 5 Easy Steps.* American Kennel Club. https://www.akc.org/expert-advice/training/teach-puppy-walk-leash/

Donovan, L. (2019b, October 31). *Puppy Socialization: How to Socialize a Puppy.* American Kennel Club. https://www.akc.org/expert-advice/training/puppy-socialization/

Donovan, L. (2022, November 8). *What Dog Is Right For Me? How to Choose The Perfect Breed.* American Kennel Club. https://www.akc.org/expert-advice/dog-breeds/what-dog-is-right-for-me/

Drake, A. (n.d.). *How to Introduce a New Puppy to Your Older Dog.* The Dog People. https://www.rover.com/blog/introduce-new-puppy-older-dog/

Elliott, G. (2022, October 4). *Kids and Pets: What You Need to Know For Safe Interactions.* The Dog People. https://www.rover.com/blog/introducing-a-dog-to-your-children/

Elliott, P. (2018, June 13). *A First Time Owner's Guide to Caring for a New Puppy.* Petfeed. https://petcube.com/blog/puppy-guide/

Embark. (2018, April 13). *How to Introduce Your Puppy to Outdoor Activities.* Embark Pets.

https://embarkpets.com/blogs/news/how-to-introduce-your-puppy-to-the-outdoors#:~:text=Some%20essential%20training%20skills%20your

Fantegrossi, D. (2018, September 24). *10 Of The Most Common Fears And Phobias In Dogs*. IHeartDogs. https://iheartdogs.com/common-fears-phobias-dogs/

Farricelli, A. (2023, February 26). *10 Impulse Control Games for Dogs*. PetHelpful. https://pethelpful.com/dogs/Impulse-Control-Games-for-Dogs

Fetch Masters. (n.d.). *Dog Socialization Problems*. FetchMasters. https://fetchmasters.com/dog-socialization-problems/

Fi Team. (2021, March 23). *10 Reasons Why You Should Get a Puppy*. Fi. https://blog.tryfi.com/10-reasons-why-you-should-get-a-puppy/

Firth, P. (2021, March 3). *The Ideal Daily Puppy Routine*. Zigzag Puppy Training. https://zigzag.dog/blog/new-puppy/getting-your-puppy/ideal-puppy-training-routine/

Flaim, D. (2012, April 16). *Teaching Kids to Love Dogs from an Early Age*. Whole Dog Journal. https://www.whole-dog-journal.com/care/dogs-kids/teaching-kids-to-love-dogs-from-an-early-age/

Flaim, D. (2016, March 11). *The Importance of Trimming Dog Nails*. Whole Dog Journal. https://www.whole-dog-journal.com/care/nail-clipping/the-importance-of-clipping-dogs-nails/

Flaim, D. (2019, September 9). *Teaching Young Children to Respect Dogs*. American Kennel Club. https://www.akc.org/expert-advice/training/teaching-young-children-respect-dogs/

Flowers, A. (2021, July 7). *Socializing a New Puppy*. Fetch. https://pets.webmd.com/dogs/guide/socializing-new-puppy

Four Paws. (2020, October 11). *Does a Dog Fit My Lifestyle?* Four Paws. https://www.four-paws.org/our-stories/publications-guides/does-a-dog-fit-my-lifestyle

Four Paws. (2022, May 27). *Fear, Anxiety and Phobias in Our Pets*. Four Paws. https://www.four-paws.org/campaigns-topics/topics/companion-animals/fear-anxiety-and-phobias-in-our-pets

Fulcher, S. (2014, January 2). *Ten Reasons Your Dog May Develop Behavior Problems*. Clicker Training. https://www.clickertraining.com/ten-reasons-your-dog-may-develop-behavior-problems

Gantt, E. (2021, May 7). *How to Set a Daily Routine for Your New Puppy*. Wagwalking. https://wagwalking.com/wellness/how-to-set-a-daily-routine-for-your-new-puppy

Geier, E. (2023, March 2). *We Review the Best Dog Harnesses for Every Kind of Dog*. Rover Reviews. https://www.rover.com/blog/reviews/review-best-dog-harnesses/

Gerrity, S. (2021, April 27). *How to Create a Pet First Aid Kit, According to a Vet*. Daily Paws. https://www.dailypaws.com/dogs-puppies/health-care/dog-first-aid-emergency/pet-first-aid-kit

Gibeault, S. (2018, April 30). *Positive Rewards Dog Training Tips*. American Kennel Club. https://www.akc.org/expert-advice/training/training-rewards/

Gibeault, S. (2020a, November 19). *Impulse Control for Dogs*. American Kennel Club. https://www.akc.org/expert-advice/training/teaching-your-pup-self-control/

Gibeault, S. (2020b, December 23). *How to Stop Your Dog from Jumping up on People*. American Kennel Club. https://www.akc.org/expert-advice/training/how-to-stop-your-dog-from-jumping-up-on-people/

Gibeault, S. (2021, June 23). *How to Make Vet Visits Stress-Free & Pleasant for Your Dog*. American Kennel Club. https://www.akc.org/expert-advice/training/make-vet-visits-stress-free/

Gibeault, S. (2022, February 25). *How to Raise a Confident Puppy*. American Kennel Club. https://www.akc.org/expert-advice/training/how-do-you-raise-a-confident-puppy/

Grayson, A. (2019, May 5). *Not every dog is a social butterfly*. Augusta Grayson. https://www.caninetraining.co.nz/blog/dog-dog-sociability

Greyhound World. (2020, December 27). *How Fast Is A Greyhound?* Greyhound World. https://greyhound.world/how-fast-is-a-greyhound/

Haley. (2019, October 18). *Adopt OR Shop: Just Do It Responsibly*. Paws and Reflect. https://pawsandreflect.blog/adopt-or-shop-just-do-it-responsibly/

Harleman, J. (n.d.). *5 Common Dog Fears and How to Help*. The Dog People. https://www.rover.com/blog/common-dog-fears/

Hartz. (2015, March 13). *How to Treat Your Dog for Intestinal Parasites*. Hartz. https://www.hartz.com/how-to-treat-your-dog-for-intestinal-parasites/#:~:text=Roundworms%20and%20hookworms%20can%20be

Hastings Staff. (2018, September 21). *8 Ways to Prepare Your Home for a New Dog's Arrival*. Hastings Veterinary Hospital.

https://hastingsvet.com/8-ways-to-prepare-your-home-for-a-new-dogs-arrival/

Henderson, R. (2023, February 25). *Top 5 Tips for Adopting a New Dog.* PetHelpful. https://pethelpful.com/dogs/Top-5-Tips-for-Adopting-a-New-Dog

Horowitz, A. (2022, November 11). *9 Best Dog Training Tools & Products Professional Trainers Swear By.* Pupford. https://pupford.com/best-dog-training-products/

Horwitz, D. (n.d.). *Overcoming Fears with Desensitization and Counterconditioning.* VCA Animal Hospitals. https://vcahospitals.com/know-your-pet/overcoming-fears-with-desensitization-and-counterconditioning#:~:text=Desensitization%20is%20a%20technique%20of

How to Train a Dream Dog. (2019, May 23). *10 Tips to Keep Your Puppy Safe.* How to Train a Dream Dog. https://www.howtotrainadreamdog.com/10-tips-to-keep-your-puppy-safe/

The Humane Society of the United States. (n.d.-a). *Positive reinforcement training.* The Humane Society of the United States. https://www.humanesociety.org/resources/positive-reinforcement-training

The Humane Society of the United States. (n.d.-b). *Stop your dog from jumping up.* The Humane Society of the United States. https://www.humanesociety.org/resources/stop-your-dog-jumping#:~:text=Teach%20your%20dog%20that%20they

Jaclyn, F. (2021, April 16). *15 Things Every New Puppy Parent Must Have.* DogTime. https://dogtime.com/lifestyle/21800-things-puppy-parent-must-have

Johnson, M. (2022, June 23). *Try These Easy Tricks To Stop A Puppy From Barking*. PawTracks. https://www.pawtracks.com/getting-started/how-to-stop-puppies-from-barking/

Jones, E. (2019, November 22). *Impulse Control Games for Dogs: Teaching Self-Control!* K9 of Mine. https://www.k9ofmine.com/impulse-control-games-for-dogs/

Jones, J. (2019, December 1). *Training A Puppy For Grooming*. Small Dog Place. https://www.smalldogplace.com/training-a-puppy-for-grooming.html

Jones, N. (2020, November 18). *How to take your puppy outside*. PetPlan. https://www.petplan.co.uk/pet-information/puppy/advice/first-steps-outside/

Karnes, M. (2016, September 14). *More Harm than Good: 3 Reasons Why I Never Socialize my Puppies*. The Collared Scholar. https://www.collared-scholar.com/more-harm-than-good-3-reasons-why-i-never-socialize-my-puppies/

Kearl, M. (2020, March 26). *Introducing New Puppies To Homes With Senior Dogs*. American Kennel Club. https://www.akc.org/expert-advice/puppy-information/introducing-puppies-to-senior-dogs/

Kelley, T. L. (2022, November 22). *When Can Puppies Go Outside? What a Vet Wants You to Know*. Daily Paws. https://www.dailypaws.com/dogs-puppies/health-care/puppy-care/when-can-puppies-go-outside

The Kennel Club. (n.d.-a). *Finding the right dog*. The Kennel Club. https://www.thekennelclub.org.uk/getting-a-dog/are-you-ready/finding-the-right-dog/

The Kennel Club. (n.d.-b). *How do I stop my puppy biting?* The Kennel Club. https://www.thekennelclub.org.uk/dog-training/getting-started-in-dog-training/dog-training-and-games/how-do-i-stop-my-puppy-mouthing/?gclid=Cj0KCQjwocShBhCOARIsAFVYq0i0e4eo-eRwyrrPpSB9Tte8CQKiLz41tb6gw5JagrViTslVD2XRx2saAjkjEALw_wcB

The Kennel Club. (n.d.-c). *What is puppy socialisation?* The Kennel Club. https://www.thekennelclub.org.uk/getting-a-dog/caring-for-your-new-puppy/what-is-puppy-socialisation/

Kilstein, H. (2021, December 29). *7 Steps to Raising a Dog that Enjoys Being Groomed.* Dogington Post. https://www.dogingtonpost.com/7-steps-to-raising-a-dog-that-enjoys-being-groomed/

Kristen. (2014, September 7). *Types of Rewards - Miami Dog Training.* Crown Dog Training. https://crowndogtraining.com/2014/09/07/types-of-rewards/

Landsberg, G. (2022, October). *Behavior Modification in Dogs.* Veterinary Manual. https://www.msdvetmanual.com/dog-owners/behavior-of-dogs/behavior-modification-in-dogs

Larese, S. (n.d.). *How to Prepare and What to Expect When Adopting a Dog.* HGTV. https://www.hgtv.com/lifestyle/family/pets/top-tips-for-adopting-a-dog

Lauren, T. (2022, March 16). *Can My Puppy Eat Adult Dog Food?* The Dodo. https://www.thedodo.com/dodowell/can-puppies-eat-adult-dog-food

Leaks, P. (2015, November 24). *5 Methods That Will Help Reduce Resource Guarding.* Puppy Leaks. https://www.puppyleaks.com/reduce-resource-guarding/

Lee, L. (2021, August 17). *Why Is My Dog Coughing, and When Should I Go to the Vet?* Good Health. https://www.goodrx.com/pet-health/dog/dog-coughing

Leicht, K. (2022, October 13). *13 Ways to Teach Kids How to Interact with Dogs Safely!* K9 of Mine. https://www.k9ofmine.com/teaching-kids-interact-with-dogs/

Leonhardt, C. (2020, April 5). *Dog Training Tools To Avoid.* Busy Dog. https://www.busydogcolorado.com/post/training-tools-to-avoid

Llera, R., & Buzhardt, L. (n.d.). *Choosing the Right Puppy from a Litter.* VCA Hosptals. https://vcahospitals.com/know-your-pet/choosing-the-right-puppy-from-a-litter

Long, B. (2017, August 24). *Basic Obedience Training for Puppies: Where to Start.* American Kennel Club. https://www.akc.org/expert-advice/training/basic-obedience-training-for-your-dog/

Lowrey, S. (2021, September 18). *Puppy's First Vet Visit: How to Reduce Vet Anxiety.* American Kennel Club. https://www.akc.org/expert-advice/puppy-information/puppy-first-vet-visit-success/

Lunchick, P. (2018, September 25). *Teach Your Puppy These 5 Basic Commands.* American Kennel Club. https://www.akc.org/expert-advice/training/teach-your-puppy-these-5-basic-commands/

Madison, J. (2013, May 6). *The Advantages and Disadvantages of Having a Dog.* PetHelpful. https://pethelpful.com/dogs/The-Advantages-and-Disadvantages-of-Having-a-Dog

Madson, C. (2023, January 5). *When and How to Start Socializing Your Puppy.* Preventive Vet.

https://www.preventivevet.com/dogs/when-to-start-socializing-your-new-puppy

Mansourian, E. (2016, June 16). *Puppy Feeding Fundamentals.* American Kennel Club. https://www.akc.org/expert-advice/health/puppy-feeding-fundamentals/

Martin, N. (2020, March 6). *How to Choose the Right Dog Crate: Your Complete Guide.* The Dog People. https://www.rover.com/blog/how-to-choose-right-dog-crate-complete-guide/

Mauran, C. (2022, May 8). *A guide to teaching children how to pet dogs.* Mashable. https://mashable.com/article/parents-teach-children-how-to-pet-dogs

Meyers, H. (2023, March 24). *Puppy-Proofing Tips for Your Home And Yard.* American Kennel Club. https://www.akc.org/expert-advice/puppy-information/puppy-proofing-tips-for-your-home-and-yard/#:~:text=Keep%20doors%20and%20windows%20closed

Michaels, L. (2014, August 12). *Pet Parenting Positively.* Dog Psychologist. https://www.dogpsychologistoncall.com/positive-pet-parenting/

Miller, P. (2021, October 28). *Dog Impulse Control Training.* Whole Dog Journal. https://www.whole-dog-journal.com/training/dog-impulse-control-training/

Nicholas, J. (2021, May 2). *Everything You Need to Know About Crate Training Your Puppy or Adult Dog.* Preventive Vet. https://www.preventivevet.com/dogs/everything-you-need-to-know-about-crate-training-your-puppy-or-adult-dog

Nicholas, J. (2023, March 1). *10 Point Checklist for Puppy Proofing Your Home.* Preventive Vet.

https://www.preventivevet.com/dogs/checklist-for-puppy-proofing-your-home

O, A. (2018, July 5). *A Minimalist Perspective, Pros And Cons Of Getting A Dog.* Break the Twitch. https://www.breakthetwitch.com/getting-a-dog/

Pachel, C. (2021, June 3). *How to Introduce a Puppy or Adult Dog to Your Children.* Preventive Vet. https://www.preventivevet.com/dogs/how-to-introduce-a-puppy-or-adult-dog-to-your-children

Parrish, C. (2022, November 17). *Buying Guide: How to Choose the Best Dog Crate for Your Pet.* BeChewy. https://be.chewy.com/dog-crate-buying-guide/

PDSA. (n.d.-a). *How to calm an anxious dog.* PDSA. https://www.pdsa.org.uk/pet-help-and-advice/looking-after-your-pet/puppies-dogs/dogs-and-phobias

PDSA. (n.d.-b). *New puppy checklist.* PDSA. https://www.pdsa.org.uk/pet-help-and-advice/looking-after-your-pet/puppies-dogs/new-puppy-checklist

Perfectly Rawsome. (2018, December 17). *NRC Nutritional Requirements for Puppies, Puppy Nutrition, Raw Feeding.* Perfectly Rawsome. https://perfectlyrawsome.com/raw-feeding-knowledgebase/nutritional-requirements-for-puppies/

Perry, S. (2023, March 22). *9 Things You Need Before Bringing Home a Puppy.* Be Chewy. https://be.chewy.com/new-puppy-checklist-9-things-you-need-before-bringing-home-a-new-puppy/

Pet Help. (2018, January 22). *Fears & Phobias in Dogs.* Animal Rescue League. https://www.arl-iowa.org/news/pet-help/fears--phobias-in-dogs/?gclid=Cj0KCQjwocShBhCOARIsAFVYq0j5NMABSRf cHig9sWEvdTosS2TuthE-6fJy5x1MJ1xYkjX2K5M_x-IaAvuREALw_wcB

Petfeed Team. (2020, April 29). *22 Ways to Play with and Exercise Your Dog Indoors.* Petfeed. https://petcube.com/blog/indoor-dog-exercise/

PetMD Editorial. (2019, July 25). *Why Is My Dog Scared of Everything?* PetMD. https://www.petmd.com/dog/behavior/why-my-dog-scared-everything

Pets in Peace. (n.d.). *Adopt or Shop A Pet: The Pros and Cons.* Pets in Peace. https://www.petsinpeace.com.au/adopt-or-shop-a-pet-the-pros-and-cons/

The PetPlate Team. (2022, June 6). *10 Things to Prepare for a New Puppy.* PetPlate. https://www.petplate.com/blog/new-puppy-checklist/

Pocket Suite. (2021, July 7). *9 Most Popular Dog Training Methods.* PocketSuite. https://pocketsuite.io/post/9-most-popular-dog-training-methods/

Pro Plan. (n.d.). *Puppy nutrition.* The Kennel Club. https://www.thekennelclub.org.uk/health-and-dog-care/health/health-and-care/a-z-of-health-and-care-issues/puppy-nutrition/

Pryor, K. (2019, April 30). *Don't Socialize the Dog!* Clicker Training. https://www.clickertraining.com/dont-socialize-the-dog

Pup Life. (n.d.). *Getting A Puppy? Prepare For The Commitment!* PupLife Dog Supplies. https://www.puplife.com/pages/getting-a-puppy-prepare-for-the-commitment#:~:text=You%20can

Pupford. (2023, April 5). *How to Exercise Your Dog Indoors: 21 Games, Ideas and Exercises.* Pupford. https://pupford.com/how-to-exercise-dog-indoors/

Puppy Academy. (2022, March 14). *Create a Daily Puppy Schedule!* The Puppy Academy. https://www.thepuppyacademy.com/blog/2020/2/3/create-a-daily-schedule-for-your-puppy

Puppy Academy. (2022, April 11). *Why Puppies Bark and How to Stop it!* The Puppy Academy. https://www.thepuppyacademy.com/blog/2022/4/11/why-puppies-bark-and-how-to-stop-it

Puppy Leaks. (2018, December 21). *10 Ways to Give Your Dog More Mental Stimulation.* Puppy Leaks. https://www.puppyleaks.com/more-mental-stimulation/

Purina. (n.d.). *Preparing for a Puppy: 10 Things You Need to Know.* Purina. https://www.purina.co.uk/articles/dogs/puppy/welcoming/preparing-for-your-new-puppy

Randall, S. (2015, August 30). *Adopting A Dog That Fits Your Lifestyle.* Top Dog Tips. https://topdogtips.com/adopting-a-dog-that-fits-your-lifestyle/

Rea, F. (2021, March 23). *22 things I wish I had when I brought my new puppy home.* Insider. https://www.insider.com/guides/pets/puppy-supplies

Reisen, J. R. (2020, July 26). *Preparing for a New Puppy.* American Kennel Club. https://www.akc.org/expert-advice/home-living/preparing-new-puppy/

Rosling, E. (2022, April). *7 fun brain games for dogs mental stimulation.* Barc London. https://www.barclondon.com/blogs/dog-training-behaviour/brain-games-for-dogs

Royal Canin. (n.d.-a). *How To Feed A Puppy.* Royal Canin. https://www.royalcanin.com/za/dogs/puppy/puppy-feeding-and-nutrition#feeding

Royal Canin. (n.d.-b). *Preparing for your puppy's arrival.* Royal Canin. https://www.royalcanin.com/za/dogs/puppy/preparing-for-your-puppys-arrival

Royal Canin. (n.d.-c). *Puppy Health & Wellbeing.* Royal Canin. https://www.royalcanin.com/za/dogs/puppy?&utm_campaign=2021-rc-za-consideration-birthGrowth-idcp19332655335&utm_source=googlesearch&utm_medium=brand-searchPaid-test2&gclid=Cj0KCQjwuLShBhC_ARIsAFod4fJxEOUBOsVGm2LXCNEDxso8cnr4YvIhJwDwx7wLQ-3I7k1cUPP2o7QaAmM-EALw_wcB&gclsrc=aw.ds

Royal Canin. (n.d.-d). *Puppy Socialisation - Puppy Behaviour.* Royal Canin. https://www.royalcanin.com/za/dogs/puppy/how-to-socialise-a-puppy

RSPCA. (n.d.). *What you need to know about puppy vaccinations.* RSPCA. https://www.rspca.org.uk/adviceandwelfare/pets/dogs/health/vaccinations

RSPCA. (2019, September 19). *How do I introduce a new dog or puppy to children?* RSPCA. https://kb.rspca.org.au/knowledge-base/how-do-i-introduce-a-new-dog-or-puppy-to-children/#:~:text=When%20it%20is%20time%20for

Sachdev, P. (2018). *Foods Your Dog Should Never Eat.* Fetch. https://pets.webmd.com/dogs/ss/slideshow-foods-your-dog-should-never-eat

Schmidt, E. (2022, October 19). *This Pet Parenting Style Makes Your Dog The Happiest And Most Social.* The Dodo. https://www.thedodo.com/dodowell/want-secure-resilient-dog-parent-way-study-says

Seymour, K. S. (2022, June 21). *The 10 Best Toys for Puppies, According to a Vet*. Daily Paws. https://www.dailypaws.com/gear-apparel/dog-supplies/dog-toys/best-toys-for-puppies

Sharpe, S. (2021, November 5). *How to Crate Train Your Dog in 9 Easy Steps*. American Kennel Club. https://www.akc.org/expert-advice/training/how-to-crate-train-your-dog-in-9-easy-steps/

Shojai, A. (2011). *Introducing a New Puppy to an Older Dog*. The Spruce Pets. https://www.thesprucepets.com/introducing-dogs-and-puppies-2805078

Shojai, A. (2020, July 10). *10 Ways to Help Stop a Puppy Dog From Barking*. The Spruce Pets. https://www.thesprucepets.com/puppy-barking-2804577

Shojai, A. (2021a, January 9). *How to Establish a New "Puppy Routine."* The Spruce Pets. https://www.thesprucepets.com/building-a-routine-with-new-puppy-2804667

Shojai, A. (2021b, August 24). *10 Expert Tips to Ground Jumping Jack Puppies*. The Spruce Pets. https://www.thesprucepets.com/puppy-jumping-and-biting-2805079

Shojai, A. (2021c, December 26). *An Insider Shares Grooming Tips Your Puppy Wants You to Know*. The Spruce Pets. https://www.thesprucepets.com/how-to-groom-a-puppy-2804810

Shojai, A. (2022, January 13). *5 Reasons Puppies Are Good for Us*. The Spruce Pets. https://www.thesprucepets.com/health-benefits-of-puppies-2804874

Small Door Veterinary. (n.d.). *Exercise Needs for Puppies, Adults and Senior Dogs*. Small Door Veterinary.

https://www.smalldoorvet.com/learning-center/wellness/exercise-needs-dog-lifestages

Stregowski, J. (2020, April 23). *Adopting a Dog? Here's How to Prepare for Bringing Home a New Friend.* The Spruce Pets. https://www.thesprucepets.com/after-adopting-a-dog-1117330

Stregowski, J. (2021, December 16). *5 Ways to Get Your Dog to Be Happy About Going to the Vet.* The Spruce Pets. https://www.thesprucepets.com/get-dog-to-love-the-vet-1118672#:~:text=Ask%20your%20vet%20clinic%20when

Sweeney, E. (2021, February 8). *Everything You Need to Know About Dog Supplements, According to Veterinarians.* Good Housekeeping. https://www.goodhousekeeping.com/life/pets/g35432790/best-supplements-for-dogs/

Thompson, M. (2022, November 2). *5 Reasons To Send Your Dog To Obedience School.* Pawp. https://pawp.com/5-reasons-to-send-your-dog-to-obedience-school/#:~:text=A%20good%20obedience%20school%20does

Truzy, T. (2022, April 12). *8 Steps to Prepare You For Your New Rescue Dog.* PetHelpful. https://pethelpful.com/dogs/8-Steps-to-Prepare-you-for-Your-New-Rescue-Dog

Vet West. (2016, March 10). *20 Tips to Puppy Proof Your Home.* Vetwest Animal Hospitals. https://www.vetwest.com.au/pet-library/20-tips-to-puppy-proof-your-home

Walden, L. (2020, August 18). *Understanding common dog fears.* Pet Professional. https://www.petprofessional.com.au/info-centre/understanding-common-dog-fears/

Ward, H. (2022, October 12). *Toys to Keep Dogs Busy.* Trusted Housesitters. https://www.trustedhousesitters.com/blog/pets/toys-to-keep-dogs-busy/?gclid=Cj0KCQjw_r6hBhDdARIsAMIDhV9heU21ALCuVjMDnd-Iz3Zxhj85Efp0-GaK--1Ag8zzqeLSBvxuhC4aAgLcEALw_wcB

Ward, H. (2023, January 18). *How to Train a Dog to Walk on a Leash.* Trusted Housesitters. https://www.trustedhousesitters.com/blog/owners/how-to-train-a-dog-to-walk-on-a-leash/?gclid=Cj0KCQjw_r6hBhDdARIsAMIDhV-FsxkUA8FbvbNiP3HbIE8eQ1Kzv8ZGVYJKglg1XPt8w-6Bo2pojP8aAiOfEALw_wcB

Weir, M., & Panning, A. (n.d.). *Instructions for Ear Cleaning in Dogs.* VCA Animal Hospitals. https://vcahospitals.com/know-your-pet/instructions-for-ear-cleaning-in-dogs

Weiss, E., Gramann, S., Spain, V., & Slater, M. (2015). Goodbye to a Good Friend: An Exploration of the Re-Homing of Cats and Dogs in the U.S. *Open Journal of Animal Sciences*, 05(04), 435–456. https://doi.org/10.4236/ojas.2015.54046

Welton, M. (2000). *Should You Get a Dog? Pros and Cons of Owning a Dog.* Your Pure Bred Puppy. https://www.yourpurebredpuppy.com/buying/articles/should-you-get-a-dog.html

Whelan, C. K. (2022, March 18). *8 tips for raising the perfect puppy.* Care. https://www.care.com/c/8-tips-for-raising-the-perfect-puppy/

Wiginton, K. (2021, July 15). *Prepare Your Home and Family for a Dog.* Fetch. https://pets.webmd.com/dogs/adoption-21/dog-prep-family-home

Williams, G. (2023, April 5). *10 Most Common Fears Your Dog Might Be Experiencing and How You Can Help.* P.L.A.Y. https://www.petplay.com/blogs/tips/10-most-common-fears-your-dog-might-be-experiencing-and-how-you-can-help

Williams, K., & Downing, R. (n.d.). *Feeding Growing Puppies.* VCA Animal Hospitals. https://vcahospitals.com/know-your-pet/feeding-growing-puppies

Woodnutt, J. (2022, January 31). *How to stop puppy food aggression: Six tips from a vet.* Pets Radar. https://www.petsradar.com/advice/puppy-food-aggression-five-tips-to-stop-it

WVS. (n.d.). *10 Reasons Why You Should Adopt, Don't Shop!* Worldwide Veterinary Services. https://wvs.org.uk/news/10-reasons-why-you-should-adopt-dont-shop

Yates, J. T. (2021, July 15). *9 things to know before getting a pet.* RACV. https://www.racv.com.au/royalauto/lifestyle-home/pets/how-to-prepare-home-for-pet.html

Image References

Freepik. (n.d.-a). *Beautiful English Toy Spaniel Dog* [Image]. Freepik. www.freepik.com/free-photo/beautiful-english-toy-spaniel-dog-pet-portrait_19866300.htm#&position=0&from_view=collections

Freepik. (n.d.-b). *Beautiful pet portrait, small dog with cage* [Image]. Freepik. www.freepik.com/free-photo/beautiful-pet-portrait-small-dog-with-cage_21249119.htm#&position=0&from_view=collections

Freepik. (n.d.-c). *Dog Begging for Treats* [Image]. Freepik. www.freepik.com/free-photo/adorable-chihuahua-dog-with-female-owner_33790736.htm#&position=19&from_view=collections

Freepik. (n.d.-d). *Dog destroying pillow* [Image]. Freepik. www.freepik.com/free-photo/smiley-dog-making-mess-floor_29652613.htm#&position=38&from_view=collections

gpointstudio. (n.d.). *Gray puppy at the vet* [Image]. Freepik. www.freepik.com/free-photo/gray-puppy-vet_12428663.htm#&position=13&from_view=collections

Helmuth, J. (2022). *Puppies playing on grass* [Image]. Pexels. https://www.pexels.com/photo/close-up-shot-of-a-puppies-playing-on-grass-12538680/

Kittle, B. (2021). *Puppy pulling leash* [Image]. Unsplash. https://unsplash.com/photos/4_0wkzDL8fE

Rachyt73. (2020). *Muddy Puppy* [Image]. Pixabay. https://pixabay.com/photos/puppy-muddy-puppy-puppy-playing-5413165/

Rawpixel. (n.d.). *Group portrait of five adorable puppies* [Image]. Freepik. www.freepik.com/free-photo/group-portrait-five-adorable-puppies_3532486.htm#&position=21&from_view=collections

Wirestock. (n.d.). *Hungry Dog* [Image]. Freepik. www.freepik.com/free-photo/hungry-white-brown-dog-with-big-ears-brown-eyes-ready-eat-bowl-full-food_28741516.htm#&position=21&from_view=collections